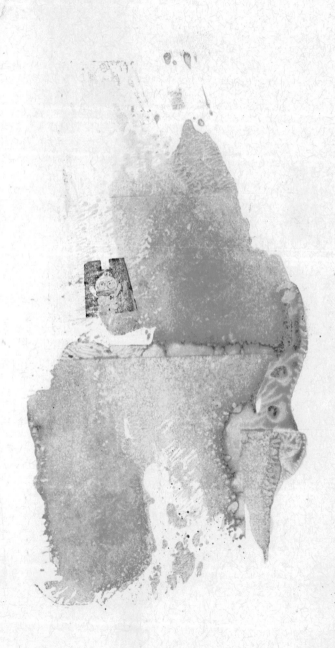

HOW TO
KEEP A MAN IN
LOVE WITH YOU—
∽ FOREVER ∽

HOW TO
KEEP A MAN IN
LOVE WITH YOU—
⮾ FOREVER ⮾

by

Tracy Cabot

McGRAW-HILL BOOK COMPANY

New York   St. Louis   San Francisco
Toronto   Hamburg   Mexico

1 2 3 4 5 6 7 8 9 DOC DOC 8 7 6

ISBN 0-07-009508-6

LIBRARY OF CONGRESS CATALOGING-IN-PUBLICATION DATA

Cabot, Tracy.
  How to keep a man in love with you.
    1. Interpersonal relations. 2. Love. 3. Marriage.
I. Title.
HM132.C32 1986   646.7'8   86-1415
ISBN 0-07-009508-6

To my parents,
Ruth and Ben Blank,
whose lifelong love has always been
a shining example

Acknowledgments

Many people contributed to the creation of this book. They gave freely of their time and shared the stories of their lives and their struggles to achieve the most important part of the American dream, a lifelong love. Some of my family, friends, and business associates gave so much I will never be able to thank them enough.

My husband, Marshall, the man I intend to keep forever, gave unselfishly, sharing his ideas and helping me in any way possible. He read and critiqued endless drafts—a thankless job. He never complained about missed vacations or having to cook for both of us, or when I became so engrossed in the lives of other couples that I neglected ours. He took care of our lives so that I could write this book. His love is my rock. My mother, Ruth Blank, whose months of computerizing, mailing, and sorting thousands of surveys from around the country smoothed my entree into the lives of so many women. Her enthusiasm never wavered even when she was buried in an awesome stack of surveys and paperwork.

My grandmother, Lillian Connors, for showing me the wisdom of her generation without censoring mine.

My dear friends Bob Leighton and Nancy Bacon, for their very special contributions and encouragement.

My technical advisor, Allen Harris, for cheerfully and patiently checking draft after draft.

My inspiration, Tony Robbins, for sharing his power.

My agents, Robert Gottleib and Irene Webb at William Morris, Inc., for their unerring guidance and feedback.

My editor, Leslie Meredith, for her invaluable input, humor, and patience.

My most important resource: Judy and Milt, Steve and Melissa, Maryanne and Bob, Ruth and Steve, Don and Nancy, Terri and Kerry, Jerry and Carmen, Carol and Ed, Phil and Bree, Marshall and Dorothy, Bernadette and Larry, Rick and Dee, Nancy and Ben, Burt and Thelma, Liz and John, William and Atoka, Wanda and Don, Lon and Rhoda, Penny and George, Tom and Lena, Nancy and Jonathan, Ralph and Louise, Patti and Henry, Howard and Carole, Liz and George, Howie and Linda, Pam and Dick, Paul and Ricki, John and Barbara, Anne and Bob, Hank and Elaine, Deiter and Andrea, Florence and Jeff, Jack and Dawn, Ian and Jennifer, David and Marilyn, Jeremy and Megan, and all the other couples who've shared so much love with me. Without their help, this book wouldn't have been possible.

Contents

HOW TO
KEEP A MAN IN
LOVE WITH YOU—
∽ FOREVER ∽

Prologue

Keeping a man in love forever is important for you if

- you feel you have made an investment in your relationship and want it to pay off

- you yearn for the deep fulfillment and security of a lifelong love

- you've worked hard at your relationship and want it to work for you

- you want equality and trust without subservience or second-rate citizenship

- you have problems with your man or relationship and want to straighten them out

- you are upset when a friend's seemingly happy marriage ends abruptly

- you want to beat the high divorce rate

- you want your man to be happy with you forever.

At last, there is a method that really works!

Introduction

HAVE you ever noticed? Couples who are truly in love, who have a lasting, universal, unshakable love, seem to communicate in an almost mystical manner. They know how to say what they want to say, when to say it and how to keep their relationship smooth, almost by instinct.

Perhaps you have seen them. . . . in church, in the park, working in the yard, or just watching television. No matter what they are doing, they seem to be connected by some invisible umbilical cord of understanding and intimacy.

You've seen him look at her adoringly and attentively, as if he were studying her and memorizing every word she says. Perhaps you've thought, If only *I* could be that cherished, that appreciated, that loved.

Now you can. The magical love a few women seem to create and maintain easily and naturally can be yours. By using new discoveries in psychology and communication, anyone can inspire, create or reignite love.

Grammar school teachers have known for years that children learn by seeing, hearing and touching. We all know that three of our human senses are sight, sound and feelings.

Recently researchers discovered that for each person, one of these senses tends to dominate most of the time. That means

3

that the man in your life is either sight, sound, or feelings-oriented. He will respond the best to one of these senses. When you know which it is, you will have the secret key to his heart, his intellect and his desires. You will know his inner "Love Language."

How to Keep A Man In Love With You—Forever will show you how to figure out your man's Love Language. Once you do, you will be able to understand what makes him tick. You will be able to instantly identify the things that will upset him as well as the things that will make him happy. You will know ahead of time what he wants—sometimes even before he does.

Once you have unveiled the secrets of whether your man is a seeing, hearing, or feeling type, you will possess the irresistible allure of understanding the inner man in ways no one ever has before—not his mother, not his ex, not his boss or his priest. You will be able to speak to him in his special "Love Language," to say the special words that will get his attention and keep it. You will be able to act in ways that will rivet his mind on you for as long as you want whenever you want. He will know that you alone are his soul mate and he'll be under your spell forever.

A few women seem to have been born with this special power to "read" and influence other people intuitively, without consciously understanding how they do it. These women were the great lovers of history, women like Cleopatra, Helen of Troy and Scheherazade. Theirs was the secret power that toppled empires and changed the course of history.

You are about to learn the secrets of these great lovers. Methods used by Mata Hari to find out soldiers' secrets, Cleopatra's and Helen's power—a power that goes beyond great beauty now can be yours.

In modern times, the people who naturally possess this gift of power show up as extraordinary successes in their fields. One of these was Milton Erickson, a therapist. His ability to establish instant rapport with patients was world-renowned. By studying how Erickson and others with this same power interacted with people, modern researchers finally unveiled these amazing techniques. Like so many great discoveries, once explained, they seem simple, easy to understand and use.

After I first exposed these powerful new ways to increase effective human communication, some people expressed concern. A few said that since these techniques were first discovered by studying how famous therapists get close to their patients, only professionals should be allowed to use them. In fact, though, others have already discovered them and use them to teach expensive seminars costing thousands of dollars—where million-dollar salesmen are taught how to get closer to their customers, and where high-priced lawyers are taught how to convince juries in huge lawsuits.

Though my methods for keeping love alive are very new, very powerful, and very effective, some people feel any methodology to assist in finding and keeping love is a violation of sacred ground. These people also probably turned their backs on computers and answering machines, airplanes and outer space. They are yesterday's dreamers, yearning for a world that no longer exists. They are usually shocked to find out that when they just let things happen naturally, nothing happens at all.

Don't be fooled into thinking we're not supposed to have to work at keeping our men. Prince Charming doesn't appear at our door and we don't live happily ever after, magically, like in a Hollywood movie. Anyone who's been in a relationship for more than two weeks knows that. Even if you're rich, thin, beautiful, and talented, you don't automatically get a good love relationship. You have to work at it. Everybody does. And that's why I believe that anyone using these psychological discoveries and techniques to get more love or to keep a love relationship, marriage, or family together is employing them to their highest and best use.

People who work at love, who don't take for granted that their relationships will last forever (and who does in today's world?), create their own happiness. And their happiness does count. Using my methods to make someone happy is not manipulative, cold, or unloving. A love that's worked at is just as vital, warm, and satisfying as one that comes "naturally." As a matter of fact, all the couples I interviewed who seemed to have an "automatically" good relationship reported that they did work at keeping their love alive.

We women have always worked at love, anyway, even if we haven't realized it. Unfortunately, the ways we have learned to get and keep love until now, by being "pretty" or "cute" or "a good cook and a good mother" or "sexy" or "faithful" don't always work in today's world. We all know at least one "perfect" wife who was unceremoniously dumped in spite of keeping a perfect figure, a perfect home, and perfect kids. And the husband always says, "She didn't understand me." Or, "We grew apart," or, "We never communicated."

Now, you'll never have to worry about hearing those words. Whiter whites, cleaner cleans won't help you. Nor will a firmer tummy or tighter thighs or even new sex tricks. But better communication skills *will*.

So for the woman who never wants to be surprised by bad news about her marriage, here are the strategic, powerful communication techniques of my "Love Plan". They are more meaningful than being "a perfect wife," more effective than having the greatest sex life, more up to date than any other techniques available.

Eventually we all get old. We lose our looks, our sex drive begins to wane. But the true love that comes from a deep inner knowledge of each other never goes away. When it's there, you are always beautiful in the eyes of your beloved.

Starting today, using these new strategies, any woman can reach new levels of closeness and intimacy with her man. Even if they've been married many, many years, she will discover exciting new ways to understand him, solve old problems, and bring him closer for a new intimacy and a mutually satisfying love relationship.

Personal Note from the Author

For years, I fantasized about the ideal marriage. I dreamed of finding the perfect man. When my Prince Charming didn't just appear magically at the door with flowers, I went out looking for him. When I found my Mr. Right, he didn't have a chance. He *had not* to love me because my unique formula for creating the magic of love was irresistible. I wrote about it in my previous book, *How To Make a Man Fall in Love with You.**

The results were immediate. Thousands of women all over the world who hadn't found love and wanted it, got it. Smart women, deserving women, women with love to give found out how to make a man fall in love. My powerful techniques helped them get the man they wanted, and many wrote to tell me their stories.

Some were divorced mothers, trying to make a living while struggling to cope with children and housework. Because they felt handicapped in meeting and attracting men, many had almost given up hope of finding a good husband.

Others, single women like me, were tired of coming home to empty houses. They were successful in many areas of their lives. They had good careers, homes, pets and investments, but not someone to love. They had spent long lonely nights wondering if anyone would ever say, "You're the one I want to spend my life with. You're the one I choose over all the others." They dreamed of white dresses and weddings and picket fences and carpools. They envied their neighbors' children and husbands. "I'd give anything to trade with them," these successful career women told me.

Now, because they learned my surefire mating methods in *How to Make a Man Fall in Love with You,* many of these formerly

* New York: St. Martin's, 1984; Dell, 1985.

single women are married. They found the man of their dreams and the commitment they had hoped for.

But they were worried. I was, too. All of us who worked so hard and yearned so deeply for so long were concerned. We wondered how we could beat the high divorce rate and keep our husbands forever. We wanted new and better relationships—with security and trust, equality and peace, and husbands who would stay with us forever. We were upset when friends with seemingly perfect marriages announced they were splitting up.

"Okay," my readers wrote me, "you told me how to get my man. I did what you said, and it worked. Now tell me how to keep him."

At first, it seemed like an easy assignment, finding out how to keep a man. Simple, I thought. Any woman can learn to keep a man in love with her. All she has to do is find out how other women have kept men in love with them for their whole lives and do what they do. So I began to ask women who had been married a long, long time and whose husbands still seemed to be truly in love with them, "How *do* you keep a man in love with you?" I asked the question over and over again, hundreds of times. And the answers were shocking.

"I keep my mouth shut," a 70-year-old woman, married fifty-two years, told me. "That's the secret, just button your lip. Don't argue with your husband. Let him be the boss. That's the way it's supposed to be and you'll have a good marriage." Woman after woman—all married a long time—echoed the same or similar thoughts and words.

Sure, I thought, fat chance. Not one of the women I knew were going to make a marriage last if keeping her mouth shut and letting him be boss was the key.

Maybe what worked for the older, long-married women I talked to had worked in the past. Maybe their advice was truly the wisdom of the ages. Perhaps these ideas would have been accepted without question by a newly married woman as recently as say, 1960. Perhaps we would all have happier, easier marriages if we just slipped into the old ways of letting him be boss. Unfortunately, even if we wanted to, it would probably be impossible. Our sense of fairness, our feminism, our desire for a say in our lives would make it so.

We women today are not like our mothers and grandmothers when they married. We are more educated. We make more money. We have more opportunities. We hold better jobs. We have birth control. We are more independent. We can survive without a man—but we don't want to. We need new ways to live *with* the men we love.

I wanted to find out exactly why some relationships worked out and some didn't. So then I decided to do research among couples who were having problems as well as those who weren't, people who were splitting up or about to. What was the problem? What were they missing? I talked to both husbands and wives. I wanted to find out what the differences were between the successful and unsuccessful couples.

Interestingly, in the broken or troubled relationships, some wives had yessed their husbands and been perfect traditional mates, others were contemporary and independent. Some had been married thirty or forty years, others just a few months. In talking to them, I found each of them said almost the exact same thing: "We lacked intimacy," or, "We didn't have good communication," or, "Maybe we never really understood each other," or, "He (she) never really knew who I was."

I was vastly relieved. As much as I love my husband, I couldn't see myself keeping my mouth shut and just letting him be boss forever. Besides, like most women today, I had sworn never to "yes" my husband the way my mothers' generation was trained to.

Soon I realized that many of my methods that were perfect for getting a man could also be used in a slightly different way for keeping him. These powerful new techniques I wrote about are better and more effective ways to understand and communicate with the one you love. Communication and understanding are exactly the ingredients lacking in marriages that don't make it and the crucial factor in the ones that do!

In spite of the fact that my original Love Plan was meant for a new relationship, not an old one, people who were dating, living together, engaged, married and even split up kept coming to me. They began to use the high-tech intimacy techniques I was teaching and they quickly got amazingly improved communication with their mates. They learned new ways of understanding and motivating their mates, ways that were not available to their mothers and grandmothers. They no longer have to "walk on eggshells" or "sit on their anger," as many told me they had been doing.

Because many of my clients realized what they had learned could be mutually beneficial, they began to share it with their mates. Both husbands and wives found new and exciting ways to look at their partners. They were thrilled by their new discoveries about each other. Even those who had been married many years uncovered new, endearing sources of delight in their partners.

I saw old battles fizzle as couples learned new, nonconfrontational ways to assert themselves and solve potential problems before they arose. Love reawakened and bloomed with a renewed respect and appreciation as each partner learned to understand and enjoy the ways in which they were different and yet the same. As husbands and wives learned to listen and talk to their loved one in new ways, they were able to revitalize their loving feelings.

By using these same new methods to keep a man in love, you can get closer to him without ever feeling as if you're demeaning or belittling yourself in any way. You can develop new personal power and self-esteem. You can learn to read your man's mind. You can uncover the secret keys to his personality and motivation. You can influence him to do exactly what you want—and he'll like doing it. You can bring back the excitement and the ardor of your honeymoon, renew the romance of days past and keep your relationship vital and loving as long as you live.

Keeping Your Man
in Love

What women should do to keep their men has undergone a complete revolution in three generations, from too many rules to none at all.

Keeping a husband happy was exactly what Tiffany, a 30-year-old psychologist, had in mind when she and Henry, a stockbroker, got married last year. That was then, now is now. "He may be just six years older than me, but his ideas of what a wife should do are right out of the dark ages," she complained bitterly.

Henry, it seemed, would only feel loved if Tiffany agreed to iron five of his polyester shirts each week. "Polyester doesn't have to be ironed." She scowled. "That's the point of buying polyester. Besides, I did not get married to be a maid. Ironing the shirts would be just the beginning. I want an equal marriage, not servitude."

Patti, married twenty-five years to Martin, a writer, is a middle-aged wife, adored by her husband. She was really angry when she heard Tiffany's complaint. Patti believes a marriage is made up of compromises. "You keep your mouth shut, then manipulate to get what you want. You don't demand. You have to decide what's important enough to battle over, and ironing shirts is just not important."

"Sure, I'd iron his polyester shirts," she told me. "If that's all it takes to keep your husband happy, big deal! So you spend two minutes a shirt and all together it would take you ten minutes a week to keep your husband happy. Any wife who wouldn't spend ten minutes a week ironing shirts if it means keeping her husband happy is a selfish bitch."

"I don't know how any of these younger women's marriages are going to last," Patti confided in me. "They're selfish and spoiled. They want it all right away and they don't want to compromise. I'll be surprised if any of them see their twentieth anniversaries."

In spite of her old-fashioned advice, "Be feminine, be perfect, or at least let him think you are," Patti vehemently denies that her marriage resembles her parents'. "My mother was totally subservient. When I ask her about how she and my father stayed together all those years, my mother tells me, 'We never had a quarrel. Whatever he told me, I did.'"

I'm sure Patti's mother did. In interview after interview, woman to woman, I found the same pattern. The older the woman was, the longer she had been married, the more subservient she was, the more willing to be totally responsible for household chores and child-raising.

The oldest of these women, the silver-haired grandmothers, were the most certain they did the right thing. The middle-aged woman, by comparison, is often seething with conflicts. She is angry about her daughter's refusal to "do for her husband." She sees it as a repudiation of "the way things are supposed to be." At the same time, she is also angry at the price she has paid, the missed opportunities, the years of keeping quiet.

For the younger, newly married woman, everything seems different. She couldn't live by the old rules even if she tried. She wants new rules for her relationship. But she doesn't know what those rules could be, let alone how they will keep her man in love with her forever.

We women today have different expectations. We want to be independent, yet we want to be able to depend on the man we love. We want to be able to stand up for ourselves, yet we also want our men to stand up for us. We want to support ourselves, yet we want our men to be supportive. And many of our men want these things, too.

Old Wives' Wisdom

After dozens of interviews with long-married women, I started asking a different question. Instead of "What did you do to keep your man in love?" I asked, "What advice would you give a young woman of today about keeping her man in love with her?"

It was a major breakthrough. The older women, it turned out, weren't really crazy about the old rules they had lived under; they were just proud that they'd made the rules work. If they had it to do all over again, many said they would do it differently. Here's their advice:

1. Maintain your own identity and your own interests. Over and over, women married many years advised having a separate identity of your own, making your own money, being an interesting person. They said, don't throw yourself totally into his life, his friends and his business. Have some activities that are yours. Your growth will keep him interested in you.

"Set ground rules at the beginning," advises Louise, married twenty-eight years to her second husband. "Don't try to be Mrs. Perfect. Know you count as a person."

"Don't make him your whole life no matter how much you love him," says Emily, married ten years to her second husband. "Don't give up your dreams, your hopes, your life to support him, because then he's happy and you're not. So then he falls in love with someone else because what he loved about you isn't there anymore and he doesn't want to hang around someone unhappy and uninteresting."

Barbara, 39, married eighteen years, dated her husband for five years before that. "I was sixteen when we met on a blind date," she told me. She says to keep a man in love a woman should "grow with the times. Be unpredictable. Keep him a little off balance. Just when he thinks he really knows me, I do something out of the ordinary." Tania, an old-fashioned wife married sixteen years to her fourth husband, says, "Stay just a little mysterious to keep him interested." Georgia, married fifty-three years to Monroe, says, "I still surprise him once in a while."

2. Don't expect to be in love with him all the time.

Couples fall in and out of love many times over the course of a relationship. Sometimes they're more out than in, but they remember the good times and hang in during the bad.

The biggest problem in relationships, according to Barbara, is: "Couples give up too soon. In a relationship, you constantly fall in and out of love with each other. Too many couples don't work at staying together." Not everything is perfect in Barbara's marriage. Her husband, Don, is definitely not romantic enough for Barbara. "I'm an incurable romantic," she says, "but what he doesn't have in the romantic department he makes up for in other ways. He helps clean the house, does laundry, takes care of the cars and yard. I can't have everything, can I?"

"The one thing missing in my marriage is sex," says Maureen. Her husband's 71 and she's 60. He's her fourth husband and they've been married fourteen years. "I've tried to get him to go to the doctor for 'pep pills,' " she says, "but he just laughs. But, boy, do we happily remember. Besides, I'm happy I met him after three previous strike-outs."

She wishes her husband would be more romantic, less of a workaholic. She wishes he would play more and work less. If she could change anything about her life she would "make more 'free' time for *myself*." (She underlined "myself" three times.)

3. Try to communicate more and better.

Maureen is sure that lack of communication is the biggest problem in marriage.

Barbara says: "Communicate with each other. Nothing is too small to discuss. We are each other's best friends. We talk and laugh a lot."

Adele, married sixty-two years to Edgar, a retired chemical engineer, was vociferous about communication. "Too many couples go through the motions, but they're not really listening to each other. They need to try hard to keep the lines of communication open between them."

These are typical responses from women married a long time. They all have some complaints. But they are basically very happy, and they have kept their men in love with them. Their advice can help guide a new generation of women in a new time.

A New Way

We all want to be women who keep our men, forever. The trouble is we don't want to do the same things to keep our men happy that women did in the past. We want the same everlasting love, the devotion, the security they got, but we want more than our mothers had. We want love and equality.

Contemporary women may not be willing to iron polyester shirts, to cook every meal or wash all the clothes, but we have what our mothers and grandmothers didn't have. With a changing society has come new discoveries in the fields of communication and psychology, and a higher level of education for women.

We can apply what we've learned during the last generation to the advice given us from our happily married grandmothers—be ourselves. And instead of expecting our men to be perfect, work to bring greater understanding and communication to our relationships.

With our new communication skills, we can keep our men happy and feeling as cared for as if we had ironed every shirt and cooked every meal. We can gain the love and security we yearn for without sacrificing our independence or feeling subjugated.

There are ways to treat your man so that you get all the love and devotion you want. Yes, you can have it all, and there is an intelligent way to go about getting it—without whining, without begging, without helplessly putting up with him the way he is or waiting for him to change.

We can have a new couplehood with new rules—one that allows us to:

- be liberated and equal yet still keep our men in love with us forever

- refuse to be subjugated and submissive yet still be sexy and adored

- make money and be independent yet still have him there to lean on

- have freedom of spirit yet have our souls locked together in love

- be caring and concerned but without feeling as if we're being taken advantage of

- give freely of our love without losing our identity

- love and be loved in spite of really understanding we're not perfect

- keep our love alive with whatever means we have.

2

What Makes Your
Man Love

S OME men like to feel they're the boss. Some make a big
deal about having their shirts ironed and their meals home-
cooked for them. Some fuss over family finances. Some are
even demanding about how you look—whether or not you're
as thin or as pretty as you used to be or always have been. If
they get what they want, they often stay married. But that's not
why they stay in love.

A man stays in love when he feels you understand him
completely—and love him anyway. When a man feels that he
can communicate with you like he can with no one else, you
become irreplaceable to him. And when you know the secrets
that can change his moods and create intimacy, he's not just in
love—he's crazy about you. Suddenly, ironed shirts, home
cooking and a few pounds or wrinkles become unimportant.

You are about to learn a proven method for keeping your
man in love forever. It starts with learning his "Love Language." If your man seems uncommunicative, or if you both
seem to be talking on different wavelengths, maybe you have
been out of tune with each other for a long time.

Your Man's Love Language

Everyone perceives his or her world by seeing, hearing and feeling. What psychologists have recently discovered is that, for each of us, one of these senses tends to be dominant. How your man reacts to you and everything else around him is influenced by whether he is dominated by sights, sounds, or feelings. This doesn't mean his other senses are not operating, but it does mean that his first and strongest reaction to something is in *one* of these senses, not all three equally.

Your man's unconscious preference for one particular sense affects his personality and inner thoughts. He is more "tuned in" and receptive in this one sense. It is his "wavelength," his Love Language.

Certain million-dollar salespersons are known for their uncanny ability to enthrall customer after customer. The reason is they are among the rare people who intuitively get in sync with a person's wavelength. Only a few people are born with this ability, but anyone can learn it.

A real estate saleswoman who came to one of my seminars would psyche out her clients by determining whether they were seeing, hearing, or feeling people. If they were visual, she'd say, "Look at the view from this house. It's so beautiful." If they were auditory, she'd tell them, "Listen to the birds sing," or "Listen to how quiet it is here." If they were feeling-oriented, she'd say, "This is a happy house." Within a year, she was over the million-dollar mark and soon led her office in sales.

Once you understand your mate's Love Language, this power will be yours. You will cross a magic threshold of understanding. You will possess a new way of communicating with his inner being, of reaching his true soul, of creating a closeness that you never dreamed possible.

Everyone who has learned these techniques—both married and single—has been able to improve their relationship markedly. Even those who have been married forty and fifty years have found greater love through new understanding.

The key to lifelong love is not physical attraction, and not ironing shirts. Understanding is the key to love and trust.

All human beings tend to be suspicious or hostile when they don't understand or trust. This holds true in relationships.

Your mate undoubtedly has at least one little trait that prompts you to say to yourself, "I just can't understand why he does that." And I'll bet that trait tends to irritate you, right? Most women shrug their shoulders and resign themselves to their mate's mysterious little foibles—"That's just the way he is, and that's that." But being resigned doesn't make the irritation go away.

When you discover your mate's Love Language, you gain an insight into what makes him tick on a very deep level. At that point, a very interesting thing happens. You suddenly understand his inexplicable reactions to things, his annoying habits and personality quirks. You know where they come from, and why. You see them as a natural, maybe even lovable, part of his Love Language.

Then, instead of being a long-suffering, passive martyr, you're in control. If his irritating trait turns out to be really lovable once you understand it, fine. If it's not, your new insight into why he can't help what he does will help you handle his eccentricities. Either way, your irritation will be replaced with understanding, and the love in your relationship will be enhanced.

Mary, an interior decorator, was attending one of my recent seminars. She complained that Mike, her husband of thirty-one years, a school principal, seemed oblivious to all her efforts to keep herself attractive and their home spotless. Recently, they had a huge argument because she threw out an old pillow. "All he cares about is having that ratty old cushion of his in his special spot on the sofa," she told me.

After hearing for the first time about Love Languages, Mary suddenly realized that Mike was really a very warm and caring type of man who experiences his world through his feelings. She learned he would always think that whatever made him feel good was most important. Since Mary made him feel best of all, she would always be most important.

"I guess I've been so bothered by Mike not seeing things the way I do that it's kept me from really appreciating him," she told the group. "I mean, he *is* the sweetest man I've ever met—and he's always sensitive to how I'm feeling. . . . And now I know! It's because he's a feelings type!"

Mary disappeared during the break. When we resumed, she confessed to the group that she was so moved by what she'd just learned that she had called Mike at home, "to tell him how much I love him."

Joan's situation was different. For years, she had been trying to get her husband, Brian, to help make the kids clean up their rooms. But he was always halfhearted about it. All he really cared about was that they turn down the stereo.

She learned that Brian was almost entirely auditory, so naturally he was bothered by the kids being noisy and hardly noticed the mess they made. "He's always more annoyed by a dripping faucet or a squeaky door than I think is reasonable," she said. "Now I know why."

In a private counseling session, Amy was distraught. "I think Ken must be having an affair," she said. "We've only been married eight months, and I'm so happy to see him when he gets home—but instead of hugging me he holds me away. He says he wants to get a good look at me, or something like that. And then I'm upset all evening."

Once Amy realized that Ken was a very visual person, it made settling into married life much easier for both of them. She found out all she had to do to turn Ken on was to let him look at her walking around the house smiling at him for a while. She's now getting more hugs than she did on their honeymoon.

Some "feelings" men, like Mike, will snuggle like big puppy dogs at the drop of a hat. "Hearing" men, like Brian, usually want to talk first and then get romantic. Others, "visual" men like Ken, enjoy looking first and then touching. It's all determined by their Love Language. Once you know what your man's Love Language is, you can easily find out what he likes and in what order.

Your Own Love Language

It takes two to tango. Making your man happy is only half the objective. You want to be happy, too.

You have a Love Language of your own. Chances are it's not the same as your mate's. It doesn't have to be for you to have a harmonious relationship. But it is very important that you learn what your Love Language is.

You need to know whether you are primarily a seeing, hearing or feeling person, just as you need to know the same about your mate. When you do, you will have a whole new understanding of how you and he can be expected to react differently. You will be able to foresee how hurt feelings, lack of sexual satisfaction, misunderstandings and bruised egos can result from your different perceptions and priorities.

You will know why you sometimes overreact to a particular situation. (You're not really crazy, you're just a feelings person temporarily trapped in a very auditory setting.) You will also be able to understand your mate's occasional strange behavior.

By understanding his behavior, you will be able to separate it from the man himself. You will be able to deal with your specific reaction to his behavior and what causes it, instead of getting angry or upset with your mate as a human being.

You can cure or change a specific behavior much easier than you can change a whole person or an entire relationship. It's easier on both of you to worry about a specific behavior that's upsetting and to change that behavior, than to try to change the basic person you are or he is.

Matching Love Languages

I have met some absolutely perfectly matched couples. One that comes to mind is a photographer and his wife, a darkroom technician. They work together side by side day by day. They are a perfectly matched visual pair. They never argue or disagree. Their values are the same, their decision-making processes exactly alike.

Then I have met other couples, also both primarily visual, or auditory or feelings, and they fight constantly. The reason for their battles is that they are so alike that they have the same exact faults. Since they both have good self-esteem, they don't get mad at themselves for these faults, but rather at one another.

Joyce and Matthew were a couple with exact matching auditory Love Languages. The problem was that neither one of them could dress correctly for any occasion without a friend to act as a fashion consultant. Instead of recognizing their own faults, each would get angry at the other.

Matthew was always criticizing the way Joyce dressed, Joyce complained bitterly to me. "He does it just as I'm about to walk out the door. When I'm late and there's nothing I can do about it, he'll say 'you look awful!' "

Matthew echoed her complaint: " I just can't stand it when she shows up looking so weird." What they didn't realize was that instead of looking at the disarray in their own appearances, each was intent on criticizing the other.

Another couple, Jeremy and Maria, had a similar problem. They were both very sensitive feelings-type people, easily hurt and very disorganized. Jeremy would yell at Maria for losing something or being wishy-washy at work. She would yell at him because he forgot an appointment or for not speaking up when people walked all over him.

They were amazed to realize they were simply a couple with matching Love Languages. Instead of seeing a fault like forgetting an appointment or being disorganized or "a softy" as something she should work on herself, Maria was quick to attack Jeremy for the same problem, just as he attacked her.

Having matching Love Languages is not a guarantee that you won't have problems. But knowing you have matching Love Languages can help you to understand those problems better.

Even if your Love Language happens to be the same as your mate's, you will not always be on the same wavelength at the same time. You are, after all, two different people. The whole point here is that having different reactions, or temporarily being on different wavelengths, is manageable if you understand what's happening between you.

Complementary Love Languages

It is statistically likely that you and your mate have different Love Languages. But that doesn't mean you're doomed to incompatibility. In fact, life can be more interesting when you bring different reactions and insights to your relationship.

I'm definitely a hearing person, and my husband, Marshall, is very visual. We both know this, and respect the difference. For us, our different Love Languages are *complementary*.

For example, when we're riding in the car with the radio on, I'll make a mental note to buy a tape of some interesting new song which, for him, is just going in one ear and out the other. Later, at home and relaxed, he'll appreciate the new music. On the other hand, I can count on him to notice a spot on my blouse before I rush out the door to tape a TV show. Which, of course, I really appreciate.

But if you don't understand Love Languages and how they work, differences in Love Languages can cause real conflicts.

Meshing Your Love Languages

Cecilia and Bob had been married just two years when she came to see me. Their marriage was in terrible trouble; they were fighting all the time. Worse yet, Cecilia was 36, ready and anxious to quit her job and start a family. Bob, at 40, was on the fast track at a computer research company and didn't seem interested in Cecilia at all.

"I don't know what's wrong with him," Cecilia, a feelings person, complained. "He's just not loving and warm, and I feel as if we're drifting farther and farther apart.

"When he comes home I go to hug him and kiss him and I can sense him pulling away from me. I have this horrible feeling that our marriage is breaking up. I worry about him falling in love with another woman and leaving me. He doesn't seem loving when he talks to me. It's as if he's shutting me out."

Cecilia was consumed with hurt, anger and suspicion. Bob wasn't living up to the kind of intimacy that she expected in their life. Even making love didn't seem intimate to her. "He just doesn't seem to care anymore. He hasn't touched me in weeks—except when he wants to get off. And then it's over in just a couple of minutes and it's as if we are strangers again."

Later, when I talked to Bob, he was really annoyed with Cecilia. "I don't know what she's talking about. It sounds like more of her complaining. Every time she opens her mouth, she's whining about something. I never have time to think."

I asked Cecilia to describe their typical evening together. It turned out that Cecilia always got home much earlier than Bob. By the time he got home, Cecilia was relaxed and starting to feel lonely.

When Bob walked in the door, Cecilia would rush to meet him. She would hug and kiss him and insist that he sit down and relax. Then she would try to get as physically close as possible, hoping to excite him into a romantic evening.

But Bob just acted as if he wanted to be left alone. He always seemed upset when he first got home, even though he loved his job. Cecilia was afraid that he was upset because he was coming home to her, so she tried even harder to get close to him.

What Cecilia didn't understand was that she and Bob were a complementary couple, with different Love Languages. She was a feelings person. He was a very auditory man. So they had different needs and responded to things in different ways.

Once Cecilia began to find out more about Bob, she was able to discover why he was such a grump when he got home. It was the roar of the freeway traffic that drove him crazy. He had a long commute and only wanted quiet time alone when he came in. It had nothing to do with Cecilia.

By finding out about their complementary Love Languages and what each needed, they were soon able to give each other exactly what they each wanted. Cecilia discovered, to her relief, that Bob's "shifty-eyed" look when she asked him a question was totally innocent—he was simply having a conversation with himself in his head in order to remember the answer. She learned to let Bob settle down after his commute and then to talk for a while before she tried to get too close. Bob needed to enjoy a little conversation, and the reassuring sound of her voice, in order to get warmed up. As soon as Cecilia understood that, she was actually quite flattered.

Bob, in turn, came to realize how important it was to set time aside for them to be together, and how much Cecilia really needed him to be physically close.

Sometimes an auditory person needs quiet. Sally, an auditory woman, was having trouble with her husband. Marty, an anesthesiologist, worked long hours, but when his workweek was over, it was behind him. He looked forward to his weekends at home. He loved to work on the house, busy himself in the garden and most of all, play with their two boys. Sally, an engineer, was also very hard-working, except for her that meant bringing some work home on the weekends.

During the week, their relationship worked like clockwork, but each weekend they almost killed each other. "By Sunday night, I've had him up to here," Sally told me. "I can't wait to get back to work. He's driving me nuts. Maybe I am crazy. He's a terrific father, and he's done wonders with the house. But I just can't go through this one more weekend."

After a short time in counseling, Marty and Sally learned that they have complementary Love Languages. Sally is the kind of auditory/hearing type who likes total quiet. Her husband, Marty, is very much a visual person. For him, it is important that the house looks its best.

Since the weekend is his only chance to work on the house, he gets up very early and starts mowing, painting, sawing, watering—and yelling and roughhousing with the kids. By the time Sally has poured her morning coffee and begun the Saturday newspaper, she is already on edge.

What they both learned in counseling was that it wasn't Marty that Sally was angry at, but rather all the bustle and noise that just naturally went with his favorite weekend things. Marty learned why all this upset Sally, to a seemingly unreasonable degree.

Soon, they worked out a schedule so that Marty would do his most noisy things when Sally was out at the gym or shopping for groceries. And he started a routine of taking the kids to a movie each weekend (a favorite activity for visual Marty). This would provide more hours of quiet time for Sally.

Sally appreciated the quiet time, and was so affectionate and happy about these changes, that Marty arranged for her to have even more peace and quiet. He bought a new dishwasher with a timer that could be set to run while they slept. He fixed all the dripping faucets in the house and took the boys to the park for wild and noisy romps.

Sally and Marty were able to defuse the problem between them quickly and easily—once they understood it. All they had to do was rearrange their schedules and change a few things around the house—a small price to pay for peace. Their relationship improved quickly with just these few small superficial changes. Neither one had to change who they are in any fundamental way.

How to Discover Your Man's Love Language

Have you ever noticed how you perk up and pick out your loved one's voice in a crowd, over loud music, almost anywhere? It's because you're tuned in to that sound. In the same way, your man is "tuned in" to certain types of communications. Learning to speak his special Love Language will assure you that he will always be "tuned in" to what you say, that your words will reach him through a sea of others, and that your feelings will always have special meaning to him.

At the same time, you will be able to influence the man you love. Once you discover your mate's Love Language, you will have the key to his decision-making process. You'll be able to positively influence him to do what you want, and he'll actually love you more for it. You'll know how to avoid arguments. You'll know the exact words to say to convince him that you are right, based on his Love Language. You'll be able to find out what's really important to him and not waste time doing things for him he won't notice or appreciate.

At this point, you may have already started to guess about what your Love Language is and what your mate's is. You may be right—but you have a good chance of being wrong, especially about yourself.

You probably have a preconceived idea about whether you are visual, auditory, or feelings, or at least what you'd like to think you are. For example, I wanted to believe I was a "feelings" woman. Since I write love books, I figured it was obvious. But I was wrong. I'm auditory.

It's always easier to figure out another person's Love Language, so start with the man you love. Don't just guess what he is. You may be surprised. Instead, read about all the different Love Languages so you can be sure of his and learn yours too.

3

The Visual Man

YOUR mate is probably a visual man, rather than an auditory or feelings man, simply because more men are visual. If he is visual, how you look will be important to him. He'll notice a new hairstyle, dress, or decor. He'll be more concerned with the expression on your face than the words with which you greet him or how you hug him.

Of course, being visual doesn't mean that your husband of twenty years doesn't really like music after all, or that your fiancé is actually an insensitive, unfeeling person.

We all see, hear and feel. Just because your man is primarily visual doesn't mean his other senses are not working. A visual man, like everyone else, may or may not have an ear for music. And he does have feelings. What's really different about him is the way his mind works. Understanding how your visual man's mind works is a way to finding out what his feelings really are.

A visual man relates to the world in terms of how everything looks to him. When he's remembering something from the past, he'll recall a picture. When he's imagining something in the future, he'll visualize it.

If you're a visual woman, you and your visual man both experience life through your eyes. You're "on the same wavelength." If you're an auditory or feelings woman, your visual man's different way of looking at things can be stimulating for you. It can also make the two of you stronger as a team. He sees things you miss. You hear sounds that go right by him.

The Visual Personality

A man who is visual is usually quick-moving. He is always bustling around doing something. It's because he processes his information mainly by using his eyes and he wants to move around to see as much as possible. Your visual man won't be able to get enough visual stimulation. He will crave it the way a baby craves mother's milk.

He's often a "type A" personality. Some people may call him a workaholic. He has high energy and lots of interests.

As long as he has something interesting to look at, he'll be happy. But he can sometimes become moody or difficult if he's overwhelmed with too much auditory stimulation, like loud music or continual chatter. He prefers movies with lots of action. Too much chatter makes him nervous.

He prefers talking about how things look; talking about how he feels can make him very uncomfortable. He finds it difficult to communicate his feelings, but that doesn't mean that he's insensitive or unfeeling or unemotional. It just means that he doesn't like to share his feelings with other people. When he's angry, he's more likely to withdraw and brood instead of getting it out.

You can get your visual man to share his feelings, but you'll have to start out by talking about how things look instead of how they feel. You can also help him out by learning to express his feelings for him and by asking questions in his visual language.

One thing that visual men hate is having their feelings spread all over. Never let him think you're talking about him to your girl friends, mother, sister, etcetera. He'll hate it but he won't say how bad it makes him feel. He'll just show his hostility in other ways.

Your visual man is very organized. He loves seeing his world neat and tidy. He can become visibly agitated when things are upset, out of place, or messy. He is sometimes considered rigid and inflexible because he likes everything just so; he isn't, but you have to know how to bend him.

He is always checking things to make sure they're right. When he drives a car, he looks in the rear-view mirror a lot and watches the other drivers carefully. He always likes to have lots of maps of anywhere he's going. If you are giving him directions, it's best to draw a map instead of writing them out.

The visual man prefers face-to-face talks, not telephone conversations, but he will respond better to written messages than to spoken ones. If you want to be sure he remembers something, write him a note.

In fact, to let a visual man know how much you love him, write him a note, leave little heart-shaped trinkets, and buy him things that he will see—like a calendar. Always write birthdays into his calendar if you want to make sure he remembers them. Give him pictures of you looking lovingly at each other.

To confirm that your man is visual and to learn more about him, start with his eyes. A visual man's eye movements are mirrors to his thoughts.

Visual Eyes

When you talk to your man, look deeply into his eyes. This is not just to make him think you're interested, which it does, or to make you look very appealing, which it also does. Look deeply into his eyes because they will make little, usually unnoticed movements.

A man or woman's subconscious eye movements are the key to what that person is thinking. No matter how old they are, no matter what language they speak, no matter what society they live in, or what their life experience or education has been, the movements are the same. They are a reflection of the passage of thought through that person's brain. He or she cannot control those eye movements all the time—that would be like trying to control their breathing all the time. It's just too difficult.

Once you learn to read these small but important eye movements, you will be able to tell what anyone's Love Language is. You will know when someone is telling you the truth or if that person is hiding something from you. You will even have some very strong clues about what he or she is hiding.

If your man is a visual man, his eye movements flicker constantly up and to one side or the other. That means he's seeing a picture in his mind. Even auditory and feelings men look up once in a while, though, so if you think your mate is visual, you will want to test him. You're looking for his initial and most consistent eye movements. Ask him some neutral questions (without visual, auditory or feelings cues) and watch his eyes. Observe his response when he has to search his mind.

For example, ask him, "Where would we go if we could vacation anywhere and time and money weren't a problem?" He looks up and says, "Tahiti."

You say, "Why Tahiti?"

His eye movements are definitely upward, but his answer is noncommittal. "Uh, I don't know."

You say, having gotten the visual clue from his upward eye movements, "Have you seen pictures of it or something?"

His eyes dart up and to one side again. He breaks into a grin. "Yeah, remember that travelogue on TV last year? Tahiti looked like a Gauguin painting. The water's so clear you can see all the way to the bottom."

You've just identified a visual man—not only by his eye movements, but also by the way he lit up when you gave him a very visual prompt by asking him if he had seen pictures of Tahiti. His answer to your question, in visual language, was the clincher. He talked about the look of Tahiti, not the sound of the wind in the palm trees, or the feeling of the warm tropic sun.

If you had asked him about seeing pictures of Tahiti and he had said, no, he didn't see any pictures, but he had heard something about it, or he just had a feeling he'd like it, you probably have an auditory or feelings man. Try again. Ask another neutral question. A pattern will always emerge.

Even if your man doesn't turn out to be primarily visual, he will visualize sometimes. Everyone looks up when they're specifically called upon to visualize something. So, whether your man is primarily visual or not, you can learn to "read his mind." Just watch his upward eye movements when questions force him to visualize.

Everyone has a pattern of looking up to one side when they are remembering something visual from the past and to the other side when they are imagining something visual in the future. This pattern holds true, even if someone is auditory- or feelings-dominated. Discover your man's own telltale pattern of remembering or imagining by watching the side he looks toward just before he answers your questions.

For example, you ask him, "What color were your grandmother's eyes?" The color part of the question forces him to visualize. He looks up and to his left (your right) and says, "I can't remember." Or, he says, "Hazel, I think." You have determined where he will always look when he's having a visual memory. That's half of his pattern.

Then, just to double check, you ask, "If we had all the money we needed for a fantasy retirement home, what would our view be like? What would we see from our front window?" He should be looking up, to the opposite side he favors when he's remembering (in this case to his right). If you go through this process several times with identical results, you will always know whether he's visualizing something from his memory or from his imagination.

VISUAL PAST, VISUAL FUTURE

"The three Rs:" A *R*ight-handed man *R*emembers a visual image on your *R*ight as you face him.

A *right*-handed man *creates* a visual image on your left as you face him.

A *left*-handed man *remembers* a visual image on your left as you face him.

A *left*-handed man *creates* a visual image on your right as you face him.

Your visual man may consistently look up and to your right when answering questions where he has to search his past memory. For example, "Can you remember your grammar school?" You have a fix on him if he is equally consistent about looking up and to your right when you ask questions like, "If you won a million dollars, what would you buy?" Now, even if he doesn't say a word, you will begin to know what he's thinking.

THE EXCEPTIONS

Some people visualize by looking straight ahead with glazed, defocused eyes. Also, you cannot always assume, because someone is right-handed, they will remember on your right when you face them. Some people are ambidextrous and some people have started out left-handed when they were young and been switched by a well-meaning teacher or parent. So always test to be sure. Some people remember on one side and visualize the future or in their imaginations about something they've never seen by staring straight ahead with dilated pupils.

Visual Breathing

A person who is visual or who is in the act of visualizing something tends to breathe with fast, rather shallow breaths rather than deep, smooth, slow breaths. He speaks from high in his chest. You may be able to tell your man is visualizing something by watching the changes in his breathing pattern as well as his eye movements.

Visual Fashion

A visual man looks well put together. He always looks neat and well-groomed. His appearance is important to him. His clothes match and he chooses them carefully.

Visual Decor

A man who is primarily visual likes his things in perfect order. He doesn't like anything hidden. His drawers are neat and arranged so he can see everything. His clothes are neatly hung in the closet, his shoes are lined up like little soldiers in military order. In the bathroom, his toiletries are always in the same arrangement.

Words the Visual Man Loves

When you talk to your visual man, you should use visual words. Visual men always respond better when you talk to them about how things look. Many women come to my seminars looking for a solution to a very common problem—"He doesn't pay enough attention to me," or "I talk to him and he doesn't listen." Because each woman is talking in her Love Language to a man who only perks up when he hears his Love Language, he doesn't tune in to her.

Visual words are easy to pick out once you start noticing them. If your visual man uses these words a lot, you should too. It's a way to his unconscious comfort level.

What Your Visual Man Is Likely to Say to You
(The visual clue words are in italics.)

I *see* the writing on the wall.

From my *point of view*, we should *look* for something else.

Do you *see* what I mean?

That *looks* like a great dinner.

Let's sit by the window so we can *see the view*.

It's perfectly *clear* to me.

I can *visualize* exactly what you're *picturing*.

I have an *image* in my mind of what it would *look* like.

I like to *observe* the stars that *light* the night sky.

When you *look* at me like that, I *light* up.

Show me where that is on the map.

Do you have a *clear picture* of what I mean?

I've *drawn a blank.*

I like to *see* you in more *muted colors.*

If I could *show* you what I mean, you would *see the light.*

When I *look* forward, I *see a bright* future for us.

I'm beginning to *see a pattern* here.

When you answer your visual man, you should use visual words, too. Here's a list of some words that will get your visual man's attention. These visual words work like magic on him.

What You Should Say Back
(The visual clue words are in italics.)

I'm beginning to *see your point.*

I can *picture* that.

I *see* how it *looks* to you.

Let's *look* through these *pictures* together.

I have a *clear picture* of what you *see.*

That doesn't *look* good to me.

Let me *see* what I can do.

Seeing your naked body makes me *light* up.

Let's hide out where nobody will *see* us.

I can *picture* us *watching* that show.

What *color* do you *see* in the den?

It would *look* better with a *shine*.

I'd like to *look* at something more *colorful*.

The doctor *shed some light* on the subject.

If I had a *clearer picture*, I could *see* what you mean.

You'll *see* how much *clearer* it will be in a minute.

I can *see* your *eyes cloud* over.

Let's get a new *outlook* on this.

There doesn't *appear* to be any *visible* difference.

Give me a chance to *look* at the problem.

Practice using visual words, especially if you are used to using more "feeling" or "hearing" words. If you usually say, "That sounds good to me," try, "That looks good to me." You are not changing what you are saying, you are just changing the way you say it.

If you usually say, "I understand how you feel," say, "I can see how you would feel that way." If you usually say, "That doesn't feel right to me," say instead, "that doesn't look right to me."

You may think that your visual man will notice if you start using words you didn't use before, like *look* and *see* and *picture*. But he won't. Those are the words that sound natural to him. He'll actually be unconsciously attuned to your every word. He'll be even more in love with you when communication becomes easier with you, and he won't know why. He'll be ready to do what you suggest because you'll be putting your suggestions in visual terms. Unless you tell him what you're doing, he'll never catch on.

You may want to share these new communication techniques with your man after you have perfected them. He'll be delighted that you have taken the time to find out new things about him. Or, you may want to keep your newfound knowledge to yourself and let your mate be happy but ignorant. Either way, the techniques work like magic.

If you're one of those women who doesn't usually communicate visually, a simple change of verbs can mean the difference between getting his attention and feeling ignored. If you are not a visual person, using visual words all the time may seem forced and artificial at first, but these are common, honest, everyday words. You can express your thoughts with them just as clearly, lovingly, and honestly as with other words.

Just a little practice and you will find that you can use visual expressions easily and naturally. You will find that no matter how many visual words you use, no matter how much you "mirror" his visual words and thinking, he'll only be more enthralled, more sure you understand the key to his inner soul. And he'll be right.

Think of the effort of learning to communicate visually as a learning experience for you, as well as a sure path to an everloving mate and personal power.

Learning to communicate with your visual mate will carry over into your other activities. By expanding your communication skills you become a more powerful person, because you are able to reach other visual people as well. You will be able to communicate better with your visual children, business associates, relatives and friends. They will unconsciously want to agree with you because you are speaking their language.

How the Visual Man Likes to Spend His Time

The following are extra clues. They should be used to verify information you've already gotten by watching his eye movements and listening to the words he uses, not as primary indicators:

Watching television or going to the movies

Vacationing where there's a nice view

People-watching at a sidewalk café

Going to art exhibits and museums

Collecting art, stamps or coins

Taking long drives on the scenic route

Reading

Operating computer games

Going to the theater

Landscaping the garden

Collecting anything classic or beautiful

Looking at you

Taking pictures

Window shopping

Looking in mirrors, combing his hair, checking his looks

Watching you try on clothes

Wondering if he matches and looks right

Watching sunsets, looking at the stars.

What the Visual Man Does for a Living

The following are more clues—secondary, not primary, indicators. These, also, should only be used to verify information you already obtained by watching his eye movements and listening to the words he uses. Your man may be very visual and not involved in any of these professions, or he could be involved in one of these and not be visual. Many men pick their profession for reasons other than its appeal to them:

Eye doctor   Hairdresser

Art salesman   Makeup artist

Filmmaker	Architect
Cameraman	Landscape designer
Photographer	Graphic artist or printer
Decorator	Advertising
Clothes designer	Publishing
Artist	Computer graphics
Sign painter	Airplane pilot
House painter	Car designer

Finding Out Exactly What He's Seeing

Once you've pinpointed your man as visual, you will want to find out exactly what he's seeing in his mind. How? Ask visual questions.

For example, you say, "Why don't we go out to the theater Saturday night with Ed and Julie?"

He says (his eyes moving up and to one side, a sign that he's picturing something), "Oh, I don't know."

You say, "How does Saturday night look to you?" or "What do you see us doing?" or "What would you picture us doing?" or "Do you see us doing something else?" He's sure to respond.

In a different situation, you might say, "Would you like Chinese tonight?" He doesn't say anything. He looks up, and he shrugs.

If he looks up on his memory visual side, then you'll be fairly sure he's thinking of some Chinese food he's had in the past. You might say, "Are you thinking about some Chinese food you had before?" or "Are you remembering the Chinese dinner we had last week?"

If he looks up on his future visual side, then you can reasonably guess he's imagining some kind of Chinese food you might eat. You could ask, "What Chinese restaurant looks good to you?" Then, if he says, "I don't think I want Chinese," you would be able to say, "What kind of food does look good to you?" or "Where do you see us going for dinner?"

If your follow-up question accurately reflects his state of mind—remembering or imagining—most men will simply answer immediately at that point. It's irresistible for him to blurt out exactly what he was thinking. It's as if a fortune-teller asked him if he was thinking about a dark-haired woman and he was. He just *has* to tell.

Influencing the Visual Man

Once you get a handle on his visual way of thinking, and what motivates him, you'll begin to understand how to influence his decisions.

You'll know that if you want new carpet, it's okay to talk to him about how good it will feel and how happy it will make you—but you're not talking his language. He'll be unmoved. Instead, talk to him about how beautiful it will look. He'll really be paying attention, and he'll be much more likely to agree.

Or, for example, if you want a vacation at the beach, he may be mildly interested in how cool it will be, or how he'll hear the sound of the waves breaking at night, but he'll be unmoved. But if you really want to sell him on the idea of a beach getaway, tell him how much he'll enjoy the panoramic view of the coast, the constantly moving waves, the blue sky and the magnificent red sunsets. Then pack your bathing suit.

One woman I know recently got new air conditioning in the house by telling her very visual husband how much cleaner everything would be. "Imagine what it would be like," she told him, "if we never had to open the doors and windows and let all that grit and dirt in the house. There wouldn't be any dust on your books and papers. Everything would stay shiny and clean-looking longer."

Women with visual men are often worried that their men

are cold or unfeeling, because these men find it so hard to talk about how they feel. Instead of demanding that he tell you his feelings, tell him how handsome he looks when he says, "I love you." Instead of demanding that he show you he loves you by bringing flowers, tell him how you always picture him when you see flowers. Visual men are moved to action if something to see is the result.

Making Love with Your Visual Man

If you're the type to spend lots of time getting yourself and your bedroom ready for love, this is the man who will appreciate your efforts. You'll never waste time getting fixed up for him. He loves to see you looking good. He'll appreciate your fashion taste.

Your visual man will be excited by what he sees. That doesn't mean that he won't appreciate his favorite music or soft sheets, but those things alone won't do it for him. He has to see something he likes.

So buy fancy sheets and pretty towels. Ask him, "What color do you think looks best on me?" Wear it. Get his opinion about patterns and sexy clothes.

If you find out he likes slinky, flashy clothes, order a catalogue and send for some. Most come with stretchy waists and one-size-fits-all measurements, so don't worry about the fit. Look through the catalogue together and ask him what he thinks of different outfits.

It's important to find out your visual man's exact sexual fantasy. Tammy and Alex had been married eight years when she decided to give him the visual surprise of his life for their anniversary. Alex was always turned on by magazines with pictures of sexy women in them. He loved looking through the sexy Frederick's of Hollywood mail order catalogue. "We ought to send for some of these for you," he'd say.

So Tammy had the wonderful idea of having erotic photographs of herself taken by her girl friend who is a photographer. The two women had great fun shopping for black stockings, garter belts and a long red boa.

Once they got started, Tammy found she really enjoyed dressing up in the sexy lingerie, and her girl friend was having a great time setting up the shots. They used *Playboy* and *Penthouse* to give them ideas about how to pose.

Then, on her anniversary night, Tammy cooked a wonderful meal. She and Alex ate by candlelight. Alex gave her a pink cashmere sweater set and a gold locket. Tammy gave Alex a beautiful robe, and then she said, "I have one more surprise for you. Wait out here and don't come into the bedroom until I call."

Tammy went into the bedroom and put on the sexy black garter belt, half bra and stockings. Next she decorated the bed with the boa and put the pictures on the bed in a large envelope with a big bow.

Alex came in and sort of laughed uncomfortably. Tammy smiled seductively and he sat down on the bed. The boa made him sneeze, so she moved it. Tammy was beginning to feel uneasy, but that was just the beginning. When Alex opened the pictures, he was furious. "I hope you're going to burn these," he said. Tammy was hurt. Alex hadn't been turned on at all and he didn't like her gift.

Unfortunately, Tammy hadn't checked first with Alex to find out what kind of sexy outfit he liked. It's very important to find out your visual man's exact visual fantasy. When Tammy really started drawing Alex out, she found that his fantasy of her was virginal and pure pink and lace—not black satin and red boas.

All visual men are not turned on by the same thing. If you find out that your husband's fantasy is to see you dressed up in some kind of sexy outfit, it's important to find out exactly what kind of outfit he means. Show him pictures. Ask him, "Is this it?" If he says no, ask him what doesn't look good about it. If he says yes, ask him what about it looks sexy.

Finding out your visual man's sexual turn-on will mean you can turn him on easily whenever you want. One woman found out that her visual husband was turned on by the color red. All she'd have to do to get him in the mood was put bright fire engine nail polish on her finger and toe nails, apply red lipstick, and then wave a scarlet nail at him . . . and he would follow her anywhere.

Chloe, a friend of mine who always loved expensive designer clothes, found out her husband was turned on by the torn T-shirt look, so she bought several Laize Adzair outfits, with the casual torn T-shirt look. For the first time, her husband didn't object to her spending money. He loved her sexy new look.

Some women object to wearing their hair in a style he loves or wearing clothes that he finds appealing. In a committed relationship it's important to please yourself and your mate. There is always a way to make both partners happy if you value the partnership.

Be specific when you ask your visual man about his sex fantasy. Ask him about his first sexual encounter, or the first time he was ever turned on. Let him tell you all about "Her." Don't worry, she's long gone. Then get him to describe her. One woman who was always worried about her weight, asked her visual husband about his very first love. Guess what? She needn't have worried. His first love was 15, buxom and slightly plump.

When you approach your visual man, always give him lots of time to look first. Don't rush up and hug him the second he walks in. Don't jump all over him until he gets a chance to see you.

The best approach for turning on a visual man is to start fully dressed, and take off a little bit at a time. Or, even while you're fully dressed, expose just one part of your body, one breast, a thigh, or some other part of your body that he thinks is sexy. My visual husband is turned on by my lips and hair, so when I want his attention I put on his favorite shade of lipstick and let my hair down.

After living with your man for awhile, you should be able to tell by watching his facial expressions whether he's turned on or not. Make a point of learning these expressions. The next time you're making love with him, watch his face. Watch for the first signs of arousal and note that expression. Observe his body language, his eyes and his actions as he becomes aroused. Watch the expression on his face when he's having an orgasm. Note each of these expressions and you will always know exactly what state of arousal he's in.

Next, begin to test. Show him a sexy picture and watch his reaction. Try on sexy clothes for him and watch his face. You'll be able to tell exactly how sexy he thinks something is. Bring home a batch of returnables and try them on for him.

Test body parts. Let him see some cleavage and watch his expression. Bare a shoulder. Flash a thigh. You'll soon discover exactly what turns him on most, just by watching carefully.

You may be surprised at what you discover. One woman found that her visual husband is turned on by the sight of her socks. "He especially likes knee socks," she told me. Later, she found out he was always excited by her plump knees, which she had always hated.

Your visual man is also going to be turned on by a special look from you. There's a specific expression you make that he can't resist. Do you know what it is? Try to remember how you looked at him when he was very loving, very affectionate, very sexy. Then, all you have to do is reproduce that expression. Visual men are very sensitive to the looks on your face. You may not even have to say a word to him to turn him on. All you have to do is smile at him in that certain way.

He will like all kinds of visual signs of your affection and sexual interest. Write him little notes and leave them where he will find them.

Keep photographs of the two of you together around the house. Make sure he has a picture of you with "that certain look" on your face. Give him a picture for his desk, one for his wallet. Make sure he can see you all the time, even when you're not around. Give him lots of visual signs of your love.

Hang pictures that he likes on the walls. Get out those

picture albums of your happy times together. Watch the expression on his face when he remembers those times. Bring out the wedding pictures, the honeymoon and romantic vacation shots. That's a surefire way to re-ignite a visual man who isn't acting loving or sexy enough.

Feed him something that looks beautiful. It's more important than good taste to him. Make sure you go to a romantic restaurant with a view.

The visual man usually likes to make love with the lights on. He wants to see exactly what he's getting before he gets it. He wants the total picture to be clear before he gets into a feeling mood.

Many women complain because their visual men don't talk about their feelings. Visual men are really uncomfortable with their feelings. They are even more uncomfortable talking about them.

The best time to get your visual man to talk about his feelings is when he's totally relaxed and completely slowed down. Like right after his orgasm. That way, he will begin to associate talking about his feelings with sexual satisfaction. Naturally, this has to be done over a period of time—gradually— for him to develop a taste for talking about feelings.

Never demand that your visual man open up and relate on a feeling level. He needs to first feel very comfortable on his visual level. If you communicate your feelings to him gradually, in visual terms, he'll begin to "get the picture," his outlook will "brighten," and he'll begin to "see" how important feelings are to you. Visual men have lots of feelings, but they find it hard to express those feelings with words.

If you want to let your visual man off the "feelings" hook, you can explain to him that you see his feelings and know he's having them, even if he doesn't express them. He will be relieved and grateful, and then you can get him to open up in a way he never has before by asking him how things look to him, not how they feel.

4

The Auditory Man

WHEN your auditory man walks in the front door, he may be totally oblivious to your new hairdo. He's mostly interested in hearing about your day and telling you about his.

He sees you, but he really cares more about what you have to say. He also has feelings, but they're not as primary to him as what he hears. Your auditory man's feelings are triggered by what he hears, where the visual man's feelings are triggered by what he sees.

An auditory or hearing man relates better to music than pictures. He is more tuned in to the inner logic of words than he is to feelings. He is easy to talk to and he loves long conversations about almost anything. Even when he's not talking out loud, he's having conversations—with himself, in his own head.

Sometimes, you might feel left out when your auditory man's having a long discussion with himself about something. But once you understand how to get into his conversations, you'll find good communication is easy with him.

The auditory man is often extremely logical, and he remembers what he hears better than others do. So be careful what you say to him; he won't forget. He'll listen carefully not only to what you say but also to what you don't say (the things

49

you leave out), and he'll be particularly affected by the tone of your voice.

Don't think you can hide things from him on the phone. He is an astute reader of vocal intonations. All you have to say is "Hello," and he knows whether you're happy or sad, relaxed or stressed.

The Auditory Personality

An auditory man tends to be more of a laid-back, mellow person than a visual man. He doesn't have to run around to "see what's happening."

His favorite activities are reading, doing projects, listening to music, and talking—often passive pursuits where he sits still and listens, or talks. Although he's usually doing something, it's hardly ever something that involves a lot of bustling around. He's more a cerebral type who lives in his head. He'll often be happy just hearing you tell him about something, rather than having to go see it for himself.

There are two types of auditory man. One is always playing the stereo, talking, or filling the silences in one way or another. The other kind of auditory person seems to hate any sounds at all sometimes (often when he's working or trying to concentrate). The reason is that any sound is an interruption of the conversation he's having with himself, particularly if it's not a sound he's chosen.

In either case, your auditory man will listen acutely and react to what he hears rather than to what he sees. His feelings are stimulated by hearing the right words said to him in the right tone of voice. As long as you are aware of his sensitivity to sounds, and know how to ask him questions in his auditory Love Language, he will tell you if he wants music, conversation or quiet.

If you want him to remember something, just tell him. You don't have to draw him maps.

Usually, auditory men will prefer talking about anything to looking at it. When he's shopping for a new car, he'd rather make lots of phone calls and find out all about the cars available and their features. The last thing he needs to do, after getting all the information and discussing it in his head, is go and look at the actual car.

He prefers talking about how things sound to how they look or feel. He finds it easier to talk about feelings than the visual man, but only because he finds it easier to talk about most anything.

Your very auditory man may hate it when you talk a lot on the phone to your friends, especially if the tone is very intimate and he's in the room. He feels as if you are giving away something that belongs to him. And remember, even if he's in the other room with the door closed, he's listening. Not a sound escapes him.

He can sometimes get upset for what appears to be no reason at all. Everything seemed fine a moment ago—and then all of a sudden he's ranting and raving. You are surprised and don't know what happened. That's because he's been having a discussion in his head and arguing for hours, maybe days or months, with himself before he even lets you in on what's going on.

Your auditory man hates screaming and yelling, especially if you do it. You can say almost anything to him as long as you keep your tone pleasant. It's sometimes infuriating to be angry with an auditory man, because the more you yell at him, the less he listens.

The auditory man is likely to be a "little professor" type who loves to tell other people how and why they should do what he says. He likes to explain things in great detail.

Women with auditory men often complain because their men are so unsympathetic or unfeeling. He's really no more unfeeling than any other man, except that he does tend to be very analytical. Tell him about something that upsets you and instead of sympathizing, which is what you really want, the auditory man starts analyzing the situation and running down all the possible solutions.

If what you really want is a hug, you will have to tell your auditory man in no uncertain terms. Thank him for his analysis but tell him, "I hear what you're saying and those all sound like good ideas, but right now, what sounds best is a hug."

An auditory man prefers long telephone conversations to face-to-face talks. He's a wonderful conversationalist and can be the life of the party when he gets started. He is often more "flexible" than the visual man just because he doesn't care too much how things look. That means he'll wear the clothes you pick out for him and let you choose the decor at home.

He has the ability to organize his thoughts into a great logical debate. Unfortunately, he doesn't organize his belongings as well as he does his thoughts. Whenever he tries, he begins to have long discussions in his head about what goes where and all the future ramifications of his choice. He never does get around to putting things in order. However, he's likely to get very fussy over picking out a stereo that sounds right.

The best way to let an auditory man know you love him is to tell him as often as possible. He needs to hear you say it over and over again. There is probably a certain tone of voice he needs to hear and a particular set of words. He wants you to say certain things in a special way.

If you don't have pet names for him, think of some. If you don't have special little things you say to him, make some up. One woman found that her auditory man responded best to baby talk, another woman found out that her man loved it whenever she called him "Daddy." Another found that her auditory man thrilled to a deep sultry tone; another auditory man loved animal noises and another foreign accents.

Auditory men often seem moody because they are so sensitive to certain noises. A squeaking chair, the clanging of a spoon in ice tea or against a bowl, or the whir of a sewing machine can set them off. If you're not auditory yourself, your auditory man's reaction may seem unreasonable, but it's not. When your auditory man gets grumpy, you can turn his mood around by switching to one of his favorite sounds.

Auditory Eyes

Just as with the visual man, eye movements are the best way to identify an auditory man. Look into his eyes, and he'll think you're really interested in what he's saying, never suspecting you're reading his mind. If you suspect you have an auditory man, be sure to say something or make little noises once in a while. Auditory responses are very important to him. That way, he feels comfortable with you.

While you're looking into his eyes, check for little side-to-side movements. These mostly subconscious movements are the key to what he is thinking and when he's having conversations with himself.

His eye movements are a reflection of the thoughts passing through his brain. He can't control them any more than he can control the beating of his heart. They are the clue to your man's Love Language.

Every auditory man looks from side to side, off toward his ears, as if he were checking with some other person in the room. In a way he is. He's checking with his own alter ego, discussing things with himself, listening to his inner voices.

These eye movements are easy to spot, if you're looking for them. When he's thinking, he'll look like he's watching a tennis match. That doesn't mean he won't look up or down once in a while, of course; it means that his dominant eye movements will be side to side.

Check his eye movements when he's searching his mind, for example, trying to recall some half-forgotten information—how to recite the Preamble to the Constitution or the

Pledge of Allegiance or the Lord's Prayer. Watch his eyes as he searches for the memory of the words. A visual man will look up and visualize the long-ago memorized material, an auditory man will look to one side and hear the words in his mind.

Or, you can ask harmless, neutral questions. For instance, you say, "Where would you like to go on our vacation this year?"

He says, "Vienna."

You say, "Why Vienna?"

His eyes flash from side to side and he says, "Oh, I don't know. I thought it would be nice" (his eyes move toward the side again).

You say, having gotten the auditory clue from his sideways eye movements, "Have you heard the ads for Vienna on the news or somewhere?"

His eyes move to the side and he smiles slightly. "Yeah, I was driving home yesterday and I heard this commercial for Austria with a background of Viennese opera singers. It sounded like angels singing. I would love to go hear that in person."

If his eye movements are definitely from side to side when he's thinking about the question, if his interest seems to perk up when you ask the follow-up question in auditory terms, and if he answers in auditory terms, you can be pretty sure you have an auditory man. If so, you are on your way to being able to "read" him like you never have before.

Most auditory men have a pattern of looking to one particular side when they are remembering something from the past, and looking to the opposite side when they are imagining something in the future. The illustrations on the next page will give you guidelines about what pattern to expect from your auditory mate. While there are exceptions to these guidelines, each person's individual pattern is consistent. Once you learn your man's pattern, you will have a good clue as to whether he is remembering sounds from his past or imagining words he's never heard before.

AUDITORY PAST, AUDITORY FUTURE

The three Rs: A *R*ight-handed man *R*emembers something he's heard with eye movements that go toward your *R*ight as you face him.

A *right*-handed man *creates* something auditory with eye movements that go toward your left as you face him.

A *left*-handed man *remembers* something he heard with eye movements that go toward your left as you face him.

A *left*-handed man *creates* an auditory experience with eye movements that go toward your right as you face him.

THE EXCEPTIONS

Remember, these are guidelines, not laws of physics. Your man may have started out left-handed and then switched to right-handed when he was young, in which case his pattern could be either of those shown above. In any case, you should confirm your own mate's particular pattern by asking him questions and watching his eyes.

Auditory Breathing

An auditory man's breathing tends to be very measured and even. His normal speaking voice is also even. It sounds as if it comes from the diaphragm—as opposed to high in the chest, as the visual man's voice does, or from the stomach, slow and breathy, like a feelings man's does.

Auditory Fashion

How he looks is never going to be as important to your auditory man as what he's thinking about. He often seems oblivious to the dictates of fashion. His personal style is more toward comfortable than chic, and he's got all kinds of reasons why he really wants new clothes just like his old ones.

Auditory Decor

An auditory man is hardly interested in decor. He'll always choose function over form when it comes to furniture placement or even picking colors. If you want to convince him that he should rearrange anything, just tell him it will be more convenient.

While his basic pattern recognition skills are not lacking, he's not oriented toward neat visual patterns. Don't expect his shoes to be lined up in a row. He probably won't put things back where he got them, since he never did really focus on what the arrangement looked like in the first place.

He can be trained, but it's not easy. And never on the basis of appearance. He will only do something different if you convince him that it will work better. So if you can't stand your old refrigerator, which no longer matches your other kitchen appliances, you can convince him to change by telling him a new fridge will save energy and run more quietly.

Words the Auditory Man Loves

Another way to tell an auditory man is by his choice of words. Auditory men just unconsciously select words that describe sounds. If your man seems to use these words in preference to those listed in the preceding and following chapters, you have further confirmation that his Love Language is indeed auditory.

What Your Auditory Man Is Likely to Say to You

Just *listening to what you say,* I can *hear* the truth.

That *sounds* like a good idea.

Let's sit *quietly* and *talk* things over.

I *hear* a little *voice telling* me to *listen* carefully.

The *rhythm* of Sunday morning is *music* to me.

That *rings* true to me.

He seems to *tune out* when I *talk* to him.

Your *voice* always *sounds* sexy to me.

There's so much *noise,* I can't think.

Let's have a little *harmony* around here.

I can *hear* you *clear as a bell.*

Let's not have a lot of *static* over this.

Let's *listen* to some *music*.

When you *say* that to me, I want to *sing*.

Everything's *clicking* into place.

Tell me what you want me to *say*.

It *sounds* to me like you didn't *hear* what I *said*.

Never just nod when you're talking to your auditory man.
Don't depend on just gazing at him lovingly, either. You have
to learn to say the right words to him. Words are the most
important things in his life. All spoken words are auditory, by
definition, but some words are more auditory than others.
Here's a list of some words that will get your auditory man's
attention. These words will stimulate his auditory senses like a
magic potion.

What You Should Say Back
(The auditory clue words are in italics.)

I'm beginning to *hear* what you're *saying*.

That *sounds* right.

I *hear* how that *sounds* to you.

Let's *listen* to this *music* together.

Let's *talk* about how we can *tune* things up.

When I *hear* the *sound* of your *voice*, it's *music* to my *ears*.

I *say* we should each *listen* more.

I can *hear* your mother's *voice* now.

Let's make *beautiful music* together.

It's as *clear as a bell*.

If it *sounded* more reasonable, I'd *say* yes.

I can *hear* from the *tone* in your *voice* that you're upset.

Let's get out of this *noisy* restaurant.

Let's get away someplace *quiet*.

I'm always *tuned in* to your *frequency*.

Let's not *rattle around* the house all weekend.

Let's *discuss* the problem.

If you find that you've been using more feelings or visual words, practice using hearing or auditory words. If you usually say, "That looks good to me," try, "That sounds good to me." If you usually say, "That doesn't feel right to me," try, "That doesn't sound right to me." You won't be changing the meaning of what you're saying in any way. You'll merely be changing the way you express yourself.

For example, if you are a visual woman, it would seem perfectly natural for you to ask him, "Would you like to watch anything special on television tonight?"

He hardly looks up from what he's reading and answers, "Yeah, I guess." And, of course, you don't know *what* that means. You're not sure he even heard you.

On the other hand, if you remember his auditory Love Language, you would ask, "How does television sound to you?"

You will have his attention. This time, he might answer, "Well, I'm thinking about it [his eyes shoot sideways]. Actually, there is a concert on tonight I wanted to hear."

You'll find that simply changing to auditory expressions can mean the difference between getting his attention and feeling ignored. Don't worry if using auditory words seems forced and unnatural at first. These are common, clear, and valid everyday words. You can express your thoughts with them clearly, lovingly and honestly.

With practice, you will be able to say whatever you want to your mate in a way that will assure acceptance. You will be able to eliminate unnecessary stress and arguments from your relationship because you will both be speaking the same language.

You'll find that unless you decide to tell him, your auditory mate won't notice anything different except that he feels understood in a way he didn't before. You may think he'll notice the changes in your expressions, but he won't. He'll just feel closer, more intimate, more in tune with you. No matter how many auditory words you use, no matter how much you "mirror" his auditory words and thinking, he'll only be more enthralled, more interested, more sure you alone understand the key to his inner soul. And he'll be right.

How the Auditory Man Likes to Spend His Time

These are extra clues, to be used to verify information you already got by watching his eye movements and listening to the words he uses, not as primary indicators.

Listening to his stereo or going to concerts

Reading (When visual men read, they see pictures. When auditory men read, they hear the words.)

Eavesdropping on other people's conversations

Listening to the television (Auditory men don't have to watch the screen to enjoy TV.)

Playing a musical instrument

Talking on the telephone

Giving speeches or talks

Teaching

Listening to lectures

Operating a C.B. radio

Writing scripts for future conversations in his head

Listening to the radio

Philosophizing

Studying

Listening to you

Recording favorite concerts or talks

Writing

Enjoying the sounds of nature, the ocean, the birds, etc.

Giving advice

Programming a computer

Talking

Arguing

Replaying conversations in his head or even out loud (and wondering if he said the right thing or imagining what he should have said)

What the Auditory Man Does for a Living

The following are secondary, not primary indicators. Your man may be very auditory and not involved in any of these professions, or he could be involved in one of these and be a visual or feelings man.

One woman was sure her husband was visual because he worked in television. He turned out to be auditory. He wrote the script for the announcers; the pictures were of secondary interest to him. Another woman thought her writer husband was visual because he wrote on a computer and watched the screen all the time. It turned out that he was hearing the words first, and then writing them down. The writing was a visual representation of his auditory sound track. Be sure to find out what your man really enjoys about his profession since that is the main indicator of his Love Language.

Ear doctor	Lawyer
Music producer	Counselor
Musician	Editor
Sound engineer	Writer
Stereo salesman	Salesman
Piano tuner	Manager
Teacher	Computer programmer
Radio announcer	Writer
Psychologist	

Finding Out
Exactly What He's Thinking

Once you've discovered your man is auditory, you'll want to find out exactly what he's hearing in his mind. It should be easy because the auditory man loves to talk. All you have to do is ask the right questions.

For example, you say to him, "Would you like to have some people over for dinner Saturday night?"

He says (his eyes moving to one side), "Oh, I don't know. Maybe." Not a helpful response, but he's thinking.

You say, "How does a Saturday night dinner party sound to you?" or, "Maybe something else sounds better to you?" or, more specifically, "We could invite a few interesting people, listen to music and talk. How does that sound? What do you say?"

If he looks to the side where he remembers things from his past, then you'll be fairly sure he's thinking of some other gathering you've had or that he's been to. "OK," he mumbles. You might say, "I can hear from the sound of your voice that you're thinking about some other party. Are you remembering the Gourmet Society get-together we had last month?"

On the other hand, if he looks to the side where he imagines things, you can reasonably guess that he's talking to himself about what might happen at the dinner party. You could ask, "What kind of conversational group would you like?" or, "Do you think the Montgomerys and the Browns would have enough to say to each other?"

With questions that correspond to his thinking, you're almost sure to get a full and prompt answer. If not, it's probably because he really doesn't like the idea of a dinner party at all. His eyes should be darting back and forth. So ask him, "If you could say exactly what we'd do Saturday, tell me what would it be. I'm all ears." He won't be able to resist telling you everything.

Be sensitive to whether his answers are vocally enthusiastic; always listen carefully to the tone of his voice. Your auditory mate has more ways of communicating than with words. His tones have meanings of their own.

The best way to get the auditory man to share his feelings is to avoid the word *feelings*. Ask him what he thinks when he hears the word *love*, rather than how he feels. Tell him how sexy his voice is when he says "I love you."

Influencing the Auditory Man

When you begin to understand your man's auditory motivation, you'll know exactly how to get him to do what you want.

For example, say you want to get new central air conditioning. You can tell him how good it will feel to be cool next summer, but he already knows that. You can tell him that the house will be cleaner, but he probably doesn't really care. What will clinch him is when you point out how quiet the central air will be, compared to the noisy window units you've been getting along with. Then you'll be cool next summer for sure.

One visual woman I know wanted her auditory husband to go on a driving-through-Europe vacation. He didn't want to go because he wasn't as interested in seeing all the scenery as she was. She was able to convince him by telling him they could avoid loud train stations and airports. Also, she added, with their own car, they could drive to out-of-the-way, quiet country inns instead of being stuck in the middle of noisy big cities. He went along because it "sounded interesting" and he loved every minute of their trip.

Perhaps you've already dreamed of a fur coat or a diamond ring. Naturally your auditory husband doesn't hear a word you say until you tell him how practical a fur coat will be, how long it will last, and how once you have it, you'll never say another word about a new coat. Tell him a diamond ring will be a good investment, not that it'll look pretty or you'll feel so good with it on your finger.

If you want perfume, tell him, "I can hear you say 'I love you' whenever I smell it." Tell him the name of the perfume— "Joy" for example, reminds you of his name, Joey. Auditory men love the sound of their own names. Say it a lot.

Be careful, though, that you don't develop a certain tone that always means you're upset or about to complain about something. Auditory types are very sensitive and can pick up on that right away. Next thing you know, you just say his name and he gets ready to fight.

Let's say your auditory man comes home from work in a rotten mood. Instead of trying to cheer him up with a drink, food or a hot bath, put on some soothing music, say special words to him, and watch how easily and quickly his mood changes.

One woman used "healing music" to soothe her auditory husband, who could work himself into a fury all alone, just discussing a problem in his head. She simply put on a Steve Halpern or Georgia Kelly album and he began to relax. Your auditory man will also respond to healing sounds, even if he's not prone to fury.

To really home in on his Love Language, watch his face and notice when he smiles or looks pleased. Try to remember whatever you said or whatever sound preceded that. Say those exact same words or make the exact same sound again later. If he responds in the same way, you have set an auditory pleasure trigger that will work over and over again. (You will learn to "anchor" that trigger in Chapter 12.)

Making Love with Your Auditory Man

Don't count on him to notice if you spend lots of time making yourself and your bedroom ready for love. So you've put on his favorite perfume and you smell good, does he say anything? No way. You've had your hair done, gotten a manicure and a pedicure, and even bought some new sexy lingerie. He just takes it all for granted. He doesn't notice the new pictures on the wall, the new flowers in the vase.

Perhaps on some unconscious level he appreciates these things, but he could easily live without them. There's nothing wrong with all these preparations if they please you, but you should recognize that your auditory man is turned on by other things.

Buy a great stereo together and then get him all his favorite music. Forget the fancy sheets and pretty undies (unless they turn you on). Find a great erotic tale, some romantic poetry, or even some old love letters. Read them aloud to him and he'll be eating out of the palm of your hand.

Actually, he's pretty easy to keep happy; you just have to say the right words and make the right noises. Try "talking dirty" to him. He'll enjoy new positions and new sexual experiences, but he needs the same old sounds.

Your auditory man wants to know you love him, and he wants to know it in a way he can hear. Finding out what exactly he wants to hear can be easy, and very important.

Anne and Howard had been married for sixteen years when she discovered he was auditory. It was immediately clear to her that she had been doing all the wrong things to get his sexual interest aroused. Of course he yawned through the most erotic movies, failed to notice when she wore the sexiest night-gowns and seemed indifferent to her touch.

"I used to initiate sex with him all the time," she told me, "but now, I just don't bother. Even if I want to, he's let me know he's not interested the last couple of times, so I just don't anymore." Not knowing what to do, Anne had sort of given up. She didn't wear her sexy gowns to bed anymore and she hardly bothered with the things that made her feel sexy—long bubble baths, lots of oils and colognes. "What's the use?" she said. "He won't notice."

Anne just didn't know the right words to say. So we began reconstructing the times in Anne and Howard's relationship when they had been close. It turned out that when they had a beach house, things were different. Howard was definitely more turned on. That was in the early seventies. They were both hippies living south of San Francisco.

"He called me 'his woman,' and I called him 'my old man,'" she remembered nostalgically. "We listened to Cat Stevens records and said 'wow' a lot." As she talked, I could see the expression on her face change. She began to smile, remembering how they had felt then.

"I guess I wasn't very liberated. All I did was shop, cook, and change the records and the babies' diapers. Howard worked and I stayed home."

For Anne and Howard, the solution to their sexual problems started when she brought home a record of ocean sounds and played it for him. Then she bought some sixties music and played it one night. "Wow, Babe" she said, unashamedly using the word from the past and reminding him how they used to call each other "Babe" all the time. "I always felt so proud calling you 'my old man.'"

The sound of the words, music, and ocean turned Howard on like he hadn't been in more than ten years. "It was like a sexual magic potion for him," she reported. "Just hearing those special expressions from the past got him excited." After that, Anne began planning weekends at the beach for them and bought tickets for sixties nostalgia concerts. Everytime Howard heard those particular sounds from their past, he got sexy and romantic.

Just as the visual man has to see something particular to get turned on, the auditory man has to hear some particular words to be turned on. You only have to find out what special sounds turn him on and you have his secret sexual key.

The auditory man likes talk, but it can turn him off as easily as it can turn him on. By observing carefully, you will soon be able to tell which sounds will make him feel sexy and which won't.

Karen and Steve were having a terrible time. Karen would come home from work just about the same time that Steve did. She would immediately launch into her routine of cooking, cleaning and washing, talking to Steve all the time. The trouble was that Steve couldn't stand the sounds of dishes clanging, the vacuum running, and the bashing of the washing machine.

No matter how beautifully she cooked, no matter what she said, he just seemed to want to get farther and farther away from her. "But I can't just stop doing anything that makes a noise," she complained to me. "Those things just have to be done!"

After understanding that Steve couldn't help the reactions he was having to the noise, Karen decided to experiment with her routine a bit. On some evenings, she would just leave the dishes after dinner, and she and Steve would read and listen to music. On those nights, Steve was unfailingly sexy, not distant. And being auditory, he never even noticed the dirty kitchen.

Once Karen was sure this strategy worked, she used her new knowledge of how to influence Steve to get him to agree to a new dishwasher—one with a time delay which would run at night when they were asleep. That took care of the kitchen, which she hated to leave messy. Together, they worked out a weekend schedule for vacuuming and washing clothes. With a little insight and some simple rearrangements, Karen was able to bring romance back into her marriage.

Test your auditory man. Play his favorite music, get in tune with him, talk in exactly his rhythm, his loudness level.

Repeat the phrases that he likes to hear, bring home a sexy record. Tell him how sexy he is. Many couples who thought their sex life had just burned out have discovered that small changes can reignite the flame.

One woman discovered that her husband was turned on by the sounds of rain on the roof, so whenever she wanted him to make love, she turned the lawn sprinklers on. They hit the bedroom windows with that sound he couldn't resist, and the lawn got greener too.

Another woman's auditory husband was always turned off when they talked about money. Instead of never talking about financial problems, she simply remembered not to talk about them if she was in the mood for love.

Your auditory mate could be turned off by the sound of a ringing telephone, the doorbell, a baby's cry or even a humming motor. One California couple I counseled had their hot tub in the bedroom. She loved it and he was frequently turned off by the grinding sound of the hot-tub heater going off and on. By moving the hot tub to the backyard, she was able to enjoy a soak without turning off her husband.

Another woman reported that she couldn't climax without her vibrator, and her husband thought the noise was like making love to a locomotive. She found a quieter vibrator and learned to let herself go vocally, which accomplished two things. The sounds of her enjoyment turned him on and also drowned out the vibrator.

Your auditory man wants you to talk to him while you're making love. Tell him how sexy he is, tell him when he's doing something right. Say, "That rhythm is perfect for me," or, "Oh, that feels so good." The more you talk to him, the more excited he'll get. He'll also be aroused when he hears the deep breathing that signals your arousal. Let him know.

You may also want to develop some phrases that always signal your orgasm. A simple, "I'm coming, I'm coming," can induce your auditory man to climax with you.

Never touch your auditory man first. He needs to be talked

to first, even if it's only a quick "Hi, sexy." Touching him in the most loving way won't move him at all unless you say what he wants to hear, and say it first.

One woman learned to turn on her auditory man by making up pet names for all the parts of his body. His little pot belly became a love mountain. His hairy chest was the Sherwood Forest which she ran through with her fingers looking for Robin and his merry men. His belly button had wrinkles in it that looked like Old King Cole. His penis was her pen pal. She had long conversations with different parts of his body whenever they made love. It got to the point where all she had to do was begin a conversation with her pen pal. "Dear Pen Pal," she would start, "I miss you so much." Then, "My, how you've grown."

Her auditory husband was enthralled with this new Scheherazade side of his wife. If they are out and she wants to start getting him in a sexy mood, she talks about her pen pal. It's their racy little secret. Only he and she know who the real pen pal is.

"I used to worry," she confessed, "that he would leave me and find someone younger and sexier. But not anymore. Who could he find who he could tell about his Forest and Old King Cole?" It's true. Her husband is totally adoring.

5

The Feelings Man

SOME feelings men are easy to spot—they are sensitive and wear their hearts on their sleeves. Others are well disguised as macho men. What is common to both of these types, and to all feelings men, is that they are basically intuitive, and motivated largely by their feelings.

For the woman who really understands her man, a feelings mate can be the easiest of all men to get along with. Whether he's aware of it or not, on some deep level he understands your reliance on the way an idea feels, he appreciates your intuition and your love.

This doesn't mean that your big, strong, silent type is really a wimp underneath; it simply means he tends to decide important things in his life by how they make him feel, rather than by how they look or sound. He will "go with his gut feel" for a situation, rather than try to analyze it to death.

The feelings man who shows his sensitivity and readily expresses his feelings, is the easiest of men to communicate with. He is a man who cries easily, is emotional and sometimes easily upset. He appreciates your sensitivity and loves it when you show your feelings.

You can often spot a feelings man by his priorities. Would he rather spend $1,000 on a new mattress or a new stereo? The feelings man will pick the mattress. Would he prefer dressing in formal clothes and going to a ball, or just hanging out in warm-ups? The feelings man always prefers hanging around in warm-ups.

Another way to tell if your man is a feelings type is by the way he greets people. Does he touch a lot? Does he hug and kiss? Or does he shake hands and talk at a distance? At a party, does he like to really settle in with one person, or is he more likely to want to meet a lot of people? Feelings men like lots of intimate touching and one-on-one conversations. They enjoy food and drink and love physical pleasures.

✳ The Feelings Personality

Whether your feelings man verbalizes his feelings or is the macho, silent type, there's nothing hidden about his emotions.

He can hardly contain himself. When he's unhappy, a black cloud descends over everything. When he's angry, he's liable to bang on tables, storm around, slam doors, and throw things. Fortunately, he is quick to make up after he cools off. When he's happy, his happiness brims over and he wants to share it with everyone around him; his smile lights up the room and nobody can resist him.

You never have to worry about whether your feelings man loves you or not. His feelings show, even if he tries to cover them up. He looks at you and the love shows in his eyes. He talks to you and you hear his love in his voice. He touches you all the time.

He may not always show it, but he worries about your feelings. He can sense when you're happy and when you're not. He relates to emotions in a very real way. If you're sad, he feels sad. If you're happy, he's happy.

The feelings man craves love and affection, lots of soft touches and physical stimulation. He is highly attuned to his body and its relationship to others. He's sensitive to the way you touch him, or don't touch him, and to how you do or don't respond to his touch.

Logic doesn't particularly move him. Nor do arguments for beauty or practicality. More than other men, he relies on a sixth sense to decide what to do.

Physical comfort is very important to the feelings man. He likes everything he touches to feel good. He can be perfectly happy in the middle of a terrible mess as long as he has his favorite comfortable chair or pillow.

Some feelings men are very athletic and like to jog or work out, usually followed by a more sensual steam or massage.

It's important that your feelings man feel good about himself. By discovering your feelings man's physical triggers (see "Keeping Love Alive," chapter 19), you can always get him to relax, even when he's most upset. If he doesn't have a physically relaxing activity, like taking a jacuzzi or having a back rub, invent one for him. Then, by rubbing his back or his neck, you will be able to change his mood almost magically.

He is more spontaneous than the visual or auditory man— more likely to do something on the spur of the moment just because he feels like it—but your feelings man can sometimes wreck your plans. He hopes you don't mind, because he just doesn't feel like going to the movies tonight after all. Naturally you want to belt him or yell or demand that he do what he said he'd do. Better to change his feelings than try to get him to go feeling rotten. He'll just ruin the evening for both of you.

Your feelings man is easily upset if he feels that you aren't paying enough attention to his feelings. He wants you to react when he's unhappy and to at least sympathize and act as if his feelings are important, if not to do something about them. Ignore his feelings and you increase his grump factor by ten.

Most feelings men also crave close physical proximity to their mate. When they don't get it, they get upset, but find it difficult to explain why.

Melanie, a successful professional fund-raiser who was always running this committee or that, had been married to Paul for eleven years. The more successful she became, the more morose he was. "I don't know what's the matter with him," she told me. "It's as if he really doesn't want me to be at the top. I think he doesn't want me to do anything but stay home."

In order to pacify Paul, Melanie would call him almost every two or three hours when she was away. They'd talk before she went to bed at night, when she got up in the morning, and several times during the day, but he was still miserable. "He's not a child," Melanie complained. "I've even offered to take him with me, but he's just not terribly sociable and doesn't like to go to meetings and cocktail parties. Besides, everyone knows me and nobody knows him. He feels like a fifth wheel."

Actually, Paul didn't really want Melanie to stop being successful, he just wanted to be near her all the time. He was a very feelings man who needed to be touched a lot. When Melanie was out of town, he missed her physical presence, something he claimed had to do with her skin or her smell or something that was missing. He said he didn't sleep well if she wasn't there.

Once Melanie realized that it wasn't her conversation that Paul was missing, she was able to make arrangements to overcome the problem. When she went away, she left plenty of home-cooked food, with the smell of fresh baking in the air. She made sure her perfume was sprinkled liberally around the bedroom, in the living room, on his favorite pillow and on his easy chair.

When he did go with her on her convention trips, she didn't try to drag him along to all her cocktail parties and meetings. Instead, she let him do his own thing, free to return to their hotel room where he could happily read or watch TV, with his favorite slippers and pillow from home and some home-baked snacks.

Actually, Paul really didn't care if he never heard the sound of her voice, all he really needed was the reassuring sensual evidence of her presence.

You will want to know if your man is a feelings man, rather than visual or auditory. Once you know, you will immediately understand him better, and, like Melanie, you will be able to improve your relationship. The best way to tell is to watch his eye movements.

Feelings Eyes

It's sometimes hard to look into your feelings man's eyes because they often are looking down toward the floor. Don't worry though, he can sense whether you're paying attention to him without even having to look at you. He may not seem to be listening either, sometimes, but that's because he has to feel everything—checking it out with his inner barometer—before he can let you know he's heard what you say.

When your feelings man looks down, it isn't a sign that he's sad or depressed, it's just a signal that he's assessing his inner feelings. Actually, most people will look down when they are asked how they feel about something. The feelings man, when asked almost any neutral question that forces him to search his mind, will look down and to his right (your left). Then he might look up, to "see" how he feels about it, or to the side, to "listen" to how he feels about it, but his initial glance downward and to the right is your clue. It is the feelings man's first, strongest and most dominant eye movement.

Ask your man to recall someone from early in his life, say, his grandmother. If he just says something like, "Oh, she was a great old gal," ask him, "Well, what do you remember best about her?" Watch his eye movements. If he looks down and to the right and takes a moment to answer, he's remembering how he felt about her. Listen carefully to what he tells you. If he says, "Her house was always warm and smelled of good things cooking," you've probably got a feelings man. He didn't tell you what she looked like or how she sounded at all.

Ask him what he wants to do for the evening. If he doesn't give you a clear indication with his answer, give him multiple choices—visual, auditory, or feelings options. For example, you say, "Would you rather watch TV, listen to music, or just hang out and relax?" The feelings man will generally give a big sigh, lower his eyes, and say with a deep breath, "Let's just hang out and relax."

If he looks down and to his left (your right), don't conclude that he is definitely a feelings man based on his eye movements.

Some auditory men often look down and to the left when they're having a dialogue with themselves. The feelings man will always look down and to his right, as shown below.

FEELINGS PAST, FEELINGS FUTURE

Unlike visual and auditory patterns, the eye movements of a feelings man will not show a difference between remembering or imagining. Researchers have tentatively concluded that this is simply because feelings are experienced in the present. So if your man looks down and to the right, you're sure he's consulting his feelings. If that seems to be his dominant pattern, you can be reasonably sure that he's a feelings man. However, the best way to be sure is to check how well he matches all of the various characteristics of a feelings man, including how he breathes and dresses and the words he uses.

Feelings Breathing

Sometimes, you can tell that a man is a feelings type just from having a phone conversation with him, so pronounced are his voice and breathing characteristics. Compared to either visual or auditory men, a feelings man's voice is slow and deep, punctuated with audible sighs. His voice, like his breathing, is from the stomach.

Feelings Fashion

How the feelings man looks is hardly important to him. As a matter of fact, his favorite clothes are old, worn, and soft. He is oblivious to fashion and thinks being comfortable is more important than anything else.

He has a whole list of fabrics that scratch and he won't wear and he wishes you wouldn't wear them either. He doesn't like shiny things, flashy things or sequins. His favorites are soft and furry, but angora makes him sneeze. He insists on washing everything three times before he wears it, just to soften it up and make it feel like all his other clothes.

Feelings Decor

Naturally, the feelings man wants his favorite pillow on the living-room sofa and a soft place for his feet. He is perhaps the biggest slob of all the men. The reason is not that he doesn't care, it's just that he's on a different wavelength. The only way you can ever convince him to redecorate is to tell him whatever you're going to do will make him more comfortable.

His idea would be to arrange everything so that he never has to move. If he had his way, the refrigerator would be right next to the living-room sofa.

Words the Feelings Man Loves

There are special words that you should listen for when your feelings man talks. His unconscious choice of words will confirm his feelings orientation.

What Your Feelings Mate Is Likely to Say to You
(The feelings clue words are in italics.)

Why don't you *soften* up a little bit.

You're a *hard* woman.

I'm just trying to let you know how I *feel*.

Don't you *care* about my *feelings?*

When you *feel* good, I *feel* good.

When you're *unhappy,* it makes me *feel* bad.

I have a *sense* we shouldn't go.

Hold on to yourself.

Let's get away from these bad *vibes.*

I *hate* to hurry.

I try to be *sensitive* and not *hurt* people.

Their visit left a *sour taste* in my mouth.

Warmth and *comfort* mean home to me.

Let's just have *close* friends.

I'm trying to get a *grasp* on it.

I don't *like* her because she seems *cold* and *unresponsive.*

I've always *felt* more *comfortable* in a *warm* climate.

When I *touch* you, it *turns me on.*

Hard times make me want to *reach out* and *hold* you *closer.*

If you're not sure he's using these words more than visual or auditory words, ask him some neutral test questions. You might ask, "What was high school like for you?" A feelings man is almost sure to answer by telling how happy or unhappy he was, how he felt. Ask him how his day was, and he'll tell you the office was hot, or his boss was mad, or they all felt wonderful because they closed a new account. If you use feelings words, you will be connecting to your feelings man's Love Language.

What You Should Say Back
(The feelings clue words are in italics.)

I can *sense* your *uneasiness*.

I *understand* why you might *feel* that way.

You must have had a *heavy impact* on them.

When you're *close* to me, I feel *secure* and *happy*.

Let's try to get a *handle* on this problem.

I *love* to *feel* your *skin* against mine.

I *feel* like a *hug*.

I *love* to *touch* your *hair*.

Let's stay home and *relax*.

Let's both *lighten up*.

I *feel close* to you when you *hold* me *tight*.

I have a *feeling* you're going to be *happy* soon.

Let's *rub* each other all over.

We'll just sit around and *enjoy being together*.

If you find you've been using more visual or auditory words and expressions, practice using feelings words. If you usually say, "That sounds good to me," or "That looks good," try switching to "That feels right to me." If you usually say, "That doesn't look right to me," or "That doesn't sound right to me," try saying, "That doesn't feel right to me," or "I'm not comfortable with that." Your feelings man is very responsive to comfort levels.

Using different words doesn't change you or how you feel. It doesn't make any difference whether you say, "I see what you mean," or "I understand how you feel." The only difference is in how the man you love receives what you say.

Since most men will at some time or other be involved with their feelings, and since you are sure to discover others who are tuned into their own feelings, learning to use expressions like "I understand how you feel" can increase your personal power. You will be able to influence some people you could never reach before.

Your feelings man will know that at last you really understand him. He will feel your love because you are telling him about it with the right words. In turn, he'll be eager to please you and will be more likely to go along with whatever you suggest when you say it in his Love Language. If you don't tell him what you're doing, he'll never catch on.

How the Feelings Man Likes to Spend His Time

These are extra clues. They should be used to verify information you've already gotten by watching his eye movements and listening to the words he uses, not as primary indicators.

Being playful and childlike

Crying at sad movies

Giggling

Getting or giving a massage

Going to growth seminars

Getting hypnotized

Eating or cooking, or just hanging around the kitchen

Smelling and tasting

Drinking, smoking or getting high

Having new experiences

Thrill-seeking

Riding a motorcycle

Playing a sport

Exercising

Sunbathing

Sympathizing with others

Gardening

Just being

What the Feelings Man Does for a Living

These are more clues—secondary, not primary indicators. These professions should only be used to verify information you've already gotten from watching his eye movements, listening to the words he uses, and the other clues above. Your man could be involved in one of these and not be feelings-oriented, or he could be feelings-oriented and not be involved in any of these.

Dentist	Restaurateur
Sculptor	Bartender
Psychologist	Public relations
Physical therapist	Sports
Masseur	Consultant
Animal trainer	Doctor
Educator	Hairdresser
Baker	Minister

Finding Out
Exactly What He's Thinking

Lots of feelings men are just the silent type. They hardly ever talk and like it just that way. Their wives have learned to either talk for them, or to do multiple-choice interviews with their silent hubbies.

I first learned about multiple-choice interviews as a Hollywood reporter for a national tabloid. The assignment was usually to get some movie star to say he or she loved some other movie star and tell why for a cover story, complete with a photo of the smiling, in-love couple.

One of the required questions was always "What do you love about him (or her)?" Since the celebrities were often just having a brief sexual fling, they would sometimes find it difficult to answer that question. Either they were totally stuck for an answer, or what they loved was totally unprintable. So I would give them the famous multiple-choice interview.

"Do you love him because he (or she) is kind and gentle?" I'd ask. "Or is it because he always says the right thing?" or "Is it because of the way you can see the love in her eyes?" Hardly anyone could resist the multiple-choice interview and I always wound up with very good stories.

So if your feelings man isn't exactly articulate, you have a way to find out what's really going on in his head. Remember to watch his eyes. When you see them move down, you'll know that he is having some reaction to you or what you're saying, even if he doesn't say anything.

For example, you say to him, "I wish your mother wouldn't come visit us. She always upsets me." He doesn't answer, but you see his eyes look down, so you know to say, "How do you feel when she comes?"

Or you ask, "What do you think about Hawaii for our vacation this year?" He doesn't answer, but he looks down. You say, "How does a warm, sunny beach strike you?" He looks down and you can see his face and body relax as he imagines how he would feel lying on a warm, sunny beach.

Or you ask, "What would you like for dinner tonight?"

He looks down and answers, "I don't know."

You say, "Do you feel like anything special?"

He smiles, looks down, and says, "Well, maybe Chinese." By asking the question about dinner in his feelings Love Language, you get a response.

Most feelings men are liable to be slow to respond if you ask, "What would you like to watch on television?" or "How does a movie sound to you?" Instead, try, "What do you feel like—comedy, drama, horror or sex?" He relates to all those feelings words and is more likely to answer.

Feelings men are good at communicating without words. Listen carefully to the tone of your feelings man's voice and watch his body language. He will often have a whole litany of sighs, each poignantly filled with its own distinctive meaning.

When he's happy, the joy shines from his face. When he's sad, he looks as if his best friend has just died—his shoulders slump, his walk is slowed, his head hangs down. You really don't need him to tell you when he's feeling sad. You just have to look.

The feelings man is at his best, in terms of communication, when you're together. When you're apart, he's not so good. Charlene shared a problem with many other wives of feelings men. Her husband, Jack, was totally absorbed by his own feelings. Charlene was a very auditory woman. She needed to hear him say he loved her at least once a day, preferably more, and he would go away on business trips and forget to call. It just wasn't important to Jack. After all, he said, "I think about how much I love her all the time. Isn't that enough?"

Actually, it's difficult for your feelings man to understand that it isn't enough for him just to feel love and devotion—he has to tell it to you or show it to you, depending on whether you are visual or auditory. It's difficult for him, but with your new-found knowledge, you can help him understand.

Influencing the Feelings Man

A feelings man is often very moody. When he's upset, he
sometimes withdraws and seems to sink deeper and deeper into
a morass of unhappiness. That's because he easily becomes a
victim of what psychologists call "neurotic stimulus generalization." What that means is if one thing goes wrong, he tends to
generalize the bad feelings onto everything in his life, and then
nothing is any good. So he becomes more and more depressed.
That's why he sometimes seems to overreact.

For instance, he throws a switch and a lightbulb burns out.
"Son of a bitch," he swears. "That lightbulb is just like everything else around here, including me. Worn out. This whole
place is falling apart, just like our lives." Soon he's discovered
that the lightbulb is just like you, the kids, the house, the dog,
his job and his boss—no good. This is your clue to invoke the
physical relaxing trigger (see Triggers, Chapter 19), and to
show him that everything isn't so bad.

"It's true," you say, getting into a state of agreement with
him (see "Mirroring," chapter 10), "the bulb is burned out, but
the house is still full of happiness, the dog minds you, the kids
and I adore you, and your boss thinks you're wonderful." At
this point you are, of course, rubbing his shoulders (his relaxing trigger) and he feels so good he begins to think everything
is good instead of bad. *You* can switch his neurotic stimulus
generalization to making everything good instead of bad.

Food can be the key to your feelings man. One woman
discovered that all she had to do to improve her feelings man's
rotten mood was cook something that smelled good. His favorite was chocolate-chip cookies. "I realized how his mother always gave him chocolate-chip cookies when he was a little boy,
and how he had all those memories of being soothed by chocolate-chip cookies.

"At first, I thought it wouldn't work. How could I whip up
a batch of cookies on a moment's notice?" she told me. "But
then I tried one of those rolls of premixed cookies you can get

at the market. They're not bad. Now, whenever he begins to get blue and sink into a big funk, I just cut up a little of that cookie dough and pop it into the oven. As soon as the smell reaches him he mellows out."

If you want to tell your feelings man something and make sure he gets it, then touch him while you say whatever you have on your mind. That's the way to get his attention and make him remember what you're saying.

You can also influence his decision making. Let's say you've got your eye on some new upholstery for your living room sofa. Your old fabric is dirty, worn, and an ugly color. Naturally, your feelings man doesn't want his comfort zone disturbed. He doesn't want anything changed. He's happy just the way it is.

He's not unusual. Most men don't like change. But your feelings man worries that changes are going to make him uncomfortable, a fate almost worse than death or wearing a tuxedo.

Don't bother telling him how good it would look or how ugly the old one is. Tell him instead how good he's going to feel sitting on a soft, plush, thick, newly stuffed cushion. Let him know he'll be happier.

You'd probably have a better chance getting him to buy you a fur coat than a diamond ring because a fur would appeal to his sensual nature. It's soft to touch and would be warm.

Perhaps you've always dreamed of a business of your own. Don't bother telling him how much extra money you could make. Instead, tell him how happy he's going to be when you are fulfilled and happy. Let him know how unhappy you'll be if you don't work, but don't hit him over the head with a threat. You'll always get more by promising future happiness to a feelings man.

Most feelings men love being told how sensitive and special they are. You may want to share what you've learned with your feelings man, or you may want to keep your new knowledge a secret, to use when you need it.

In any event, use feelings words a lot. Touch him all the time. When you make him feel good, he'll return the favor. His happy vibes will spill over everywhere.

Making Love with Your Feelings Man

Your feelings man will love softly textured fabrics like satin, velvet and fur. He likes to feel your soft hands roaming everywhere. He can be turned on by just about anything you want to do, so let your imagination run wild with him. Be inventive. The more new sensations you can create for your feelings man, the more he will adore you.

Jane and Max had been married twelve years, and the key to their mutual sexual satisfaction had eluded her.

Jane was a fastidious housekeeper who felt she was keeping a perfect house, but Max wasn't keeping up his side of the marital duties. "I am always the one who wants more sex," she told me. "I wear the prettiest, sexiest nighties, but he always wants to just lie there and hold me and be affectionate and playful. It's driving me crazy. I really love Max and I don't want anybody else, but lately I've been thinking about it," she confessed to me.

Together Jane and I figured out that Max was a feelings man, while she was very visual. We decided that sex didn't have to be totally serious for them to enjoy it, so we devised a plan for making their sex life playful and filled with new sensations. Jane would order a vibrator, some exotic lubricant, and other paraphernalia from a mail-order book, and she would also forget the nighties and go to bed naked, like she did when they were just married. "I don't think that will look very sexy," she worried. "I've gained so much weight."

"Does that bother Max?" I asked.

"He says he loves my soft, squeezy parts. That's the trouble. He just wants to snuggle me."

I told her not to worry, and not to wait until her mail order arrived, but to use what she already had. The next night, Jane was all ready. She slunk into the bedroom, with nothing on under her robe but Max's favorite perfume, and, of course, Max just turned off the light. But, instead of giving up, Jane slipped out of her robe and into bed, lit a candle on the night table and began to run her hands all over his chest.

Max couldn't resist. He reached out to snuggle Jane, but before he could, she offered him one of his favorite Godiva Park chocolate bars. He was in heaven, holding onto Jane's breast with one hand, eating his favorite food with the other.

Soon, the chocolate was gone. "I really do love those things," he sighed.

"There's only one left, and you have to find it," she teased. By the time Max discovered the hidden chocolate buried under Jane's breast, where it had begun to melt he was totally sensually aroused, but his sense of play remained as he licked it off.

"Before, I guess I would have been too busy cleaning up the chocolate to have enjoyed the whole thing," she confessed, "but instead, I tried to get into my own feelings and ignored the mess. I was surprised. It was fun to just dive in and enjoy the game of hiding the chocolate. Then, Max wanted to eat it off. You should have seen the mess, but the sex was great. I didn't even get up to wash the chocolate off before I went to sleep."

By ignoring her urge to clean and indulging in Max's more sensual mess, Jane was able to revive their sex life and add a new dimension to her own experience.

Another couple, Sandy, a stockbroker, and Jeff, a personnel director, had been married eight years when Sandy came to see me. "He's driving me crazy," she said. "He just acts depressed and sighs a lot when I bring up the subject of sex. We haven't made love more than two times this month, and I'm fed up with it. Our sex life is getting worse and worse."

Sandy had tried just about everything—sexy music, erotic movies, books, even ignoring him, but nothing worked. She was desperate. "I'm only thirty-two. I'm not ready to give up sex for the rest of my life. I love Jeff, but I have needs. I get so nervous, I can't stand it."

I talked to Sandy about the times when their relationship had been good. I asked her, "What did you do together when Jeff was more sexual?" We discovered that the last time their lovemaking had been really terrific was three years earlier when Jeff and Sandy were living in Seattle, not Los Angeles. Their life in Seattle was totally different.

"We lived about two hours out of town. It was a long commute but we both loved the country. Weekends we would often camp out in the woods and not see anyone for days. We hiked side by side and worked side by side and slept together in a double down sleeping bag. Jeff used to say I was his Mountain Mama. We'd hike all day, get all sweaty and dirty and make love under the trees at night."

In order to re-create the feelings Jeff had when they were really happy and turned on to each other, Sandy made plans for them to go camping, something they hadn't done for years. "I brought out the old hiking boots and the sleeping bag, the backpacks and tent, and began working to organize our equipment in the living room. When Jeff got home from work, he began to help me out. We worked for hours, scrubbing our old cooking utensils and repacking our gear. We were physically wiped out, but suddenly he got turned on. We made love on the sleeping bag, right there on the living-room floor.

"It was like magic. Working together, smelling the old camping gear and just thinking about getting away, got Jeff all excited."

Sandy and Jeff, both working so hard at different careers, were totally ignoring the activities that had brought them together in the first place. It wasn't just camping out, it was working together to accomplish a common goal. And for Jeff, a feelings man, it was the smells and the sensations. He was excited by exercise, sweat and physical proximity.

They went camping once or twice, but Sandy decided a long-range project was called for. She got plans for a house addition they'd been talking about, and each weekend they worked on it. Almost as soon as they finished, like clockwork, they made love—dirty, sweaty, but fulfilled.

Sandy soon learned to forget her usual shower and just get on with it. "Anytime I want," she said, "I simply get him to work up a sweat in the garden or building our addition and afterwards we have the most exciting evening. I even bought a down bedcover just like our sleeping bag. When we're under it together it's just like being out in the woods. I realized I can always shower later."

Just as the visual man is aroused by something he sees, and the auditory man is aroused by something he hears, feelings men are excited by certain sensations. For your feelings man, sex means sensation—touch, taste and smells. Perhaps the smell of candles or incense excites him. Maybe the special aroma of your body is the key to his arousal. Even certain foods can be the key to elevating his amorous feelings. Often it's a special touch, perhaps a special way you rub the back of his neck or the way you touch his face or perhaps a kiss in a particularly sensitive spot. You only have to find out what special sense he needs stimulated to turn on your feelings man whenever you want.

"Have you hugged your hubby today?" refers to your feelings man who needs a hug to sense your love. The wrong type of touch, by the way, can turn off your feelings man just as much as the right one can turn him on.

A feelings man likes changes even less than other men. Changes upset him. If you've always slept together one way, sleeping on the other side of the bed is enough to undermine his security.

Sam and Rose had been married twenty-two years when Rose started having menopausal hot flashes. After all those years of going to sleep in each other's arms, suddenly Rose couldn't stand Sam next to her in bed.

"His body is so hot, it starts me off," she said.

Poor Sam was feeling terribly unloved until Rose discovered that by changing her diet she could alleviate her flashes.

Sam, for his part, learned to sense when Rose was uncomfortable and he'd blow gently on the back of her neck to cool her down. "Just having me close was really important to him," Rose found out.

If your feelings man isn't as sensual as you want him to be, there's definitely something wrong. Feelings men are usually very sexy. So think back to when you and he were totally in sync and try to re-create the smells, tastes, and feelings he had then. You'll be surprised to discover how easy it is to have a sexy husband whenever you want. Sometimes, just a small change can mean the difference between having a comfortable and sexy feelings man or an uncomfortable, upset one.

Test your feelings man. Touch him in "that certain way," hug him a lot, get into his slowed-down rhythm. His idea of sexy is slow and sensual with lots of touching. If you sense he's not comfortable, don't try to rush him into sex, and never get into a long intellectual discussion with him about sex. Try to communicate your feelings nonverbally.

One woman discovered that her feelings husband was most turned on by the smell of baby powder. She figured out all kinds of ways to use it, on the sheets, between her toes, everywhere in the bedroom.

Another woman's feelings husband was turned off by the smell of her new cologne. Thinking back, she remembered when he gave her a certain cologne years before. When she wore it again, he turned into his old sexy self.

One woman discovered her feelings man used to be excited by her long hair. She bought a wig and surprised him with it one night. He was thrilled.

If you haven't got special ways to touch your feelings man, think of some. Be creative. Make him feel special. One woman got to be an expert with massage oils. She had different ones that represented different moods: floral for light and easy touching, an exotic patchouli oil for wild and fantasy sex, and a cherry-scented one for when she wanted him to take the lead and treat her like a precious virgin.

"We play out different scenes to go with different smells. I even bought an antiseptic-smelling oil once and told him we were going to play doctor. He loved it. Now whenever I want to turn him on, I just bring out a certain smell and he can't resist. When we spend a night away from home, I bring along a little vial of exotic smelling oil and we make up a fantasy sex game to go with it."

Find ways to signal sex to your feelings man when you're out somewhere together, something to trigger his anticipation. Perhaps a special scent, a particular taste, or even a touch he only gets from you.

Always touch your feelings man and talk about your emotions and feelings with him. Say, "I understand how you feel and I feel the same way." It's a magic mantra for any woman involved with a feelings man.

6

The Visual Woman

AS a visual woman, you know innately what kinds of clothes look good on you. You are always well dressed and may work in fashion. Your friends ask you what to wear when they don't know. You seem to know what jewelry looks right with which outfits, and your style sense is acute. You are able to go against the fashion dictates and still look good because you have your own sense of flair and fads don't affect you.

My very good friend, who is visual, has an uncanny way of fixing whatever I have on to look right. When she arrives for our lunch dates, she can make me look stylish in whatever I'm wearing. She rolls my pants cuffs and shirt sleeves to exactly the right length, makes my collars stand up like a fashion model's, and by just changing the earrings I have on, she can transform my whole outfit. When she arrives I'm dressed, but after a couple of quick adjustments, she can make me look fashionably dressed. I wouldn't think of going on a promotion tour without first consulting with her about my wardrobe. She knows intuitively what I should wear on a London BBC program, or on "Donahue," or at an Irish country fair.

My visual friend can take the simplest dust collector and make it into a decorative household accessory. Things I might put in the trash become gorgeous after she tinkers with them.

In her hands, an old milk can spray-painted just the right color and put in just the right place becomes an eye-stopping umbrella rack. An old step table becomes a garden planter. An old lamp with a new shade becomes an area divider.

She remembers every movie she's ever seen. She knows the faces of all the stars and can recall their best scenes.

Whenever I see her, she looks good. If she's cooking, her apron is tied adorably and the scarf around her head looks like a stylish turban. When she works in the garden, even her gloves are chic. I have seen her look good taking kids to the doctor, dogs to the vet, even scrubbing floors and painting walls.

I have never seen her house in the kind of disorder mine can achieve, and I have never seen her without a manicure or with a chipped nail. No matter where she goes, people look at her because there is something striking in the casual but stylish way she manages to look good, anywhere. Even her kids show signs of her unfailing visual eye. They are clean. They match.

Visual Woman/Visual Man

If you are a visual woman, you'll have little trouble relating to a visual man. You will both want to see everything looking right. You will easily convince him to buy a new camera—pictures are important to him. You won't have to battle to paint or redecorate, because he thinks those things are important too.

Just because you are both visual doesn't mean that you will always have the same vision, however. And when two visual people disagree on the color of their living room, it can be a disagreement between experts, each of whom feels strongly they know what's best. You will want to minimize the number of such situations by discussing and agreeing on major visual changes in your life well ahead of time. Your mutual ability to imagine how the change might look will help you do this. If you can't avoid the disagreement, being on the same wavelength should help in picking a respected friend or color consultant to settle matters.

Two visual people can become dissatisfied with each other unless they stay firmly grounded in reality. Your visual man can imagine the perfect wife in his mind. He can see her clearly. Then he expects the real you to live up to the fantasy wife he pictures. Like a Stepford wife, she's not real. Naturally, you can't live up to his fantasy of perfection. Bring him back to earth by talking about other real wives when he starts comparing you to some fantasy.

On the other hand, you may compare him to your vision of the perfect Stepford hubby. If you must make comparisons— and who can resist?—be sure to compare your man to other real men, not imagined ones.

Your visual man loves that you always look terrific, and enjoys showing you off to his friends and business associates. He appreciates the way you make your home look so attractive, the way you serve food that looks visually appetizing as well as tasting good.

He's happy to let you fuss over him and make him look as handsome as you look beautiful. He enjoys looking at you and it's important to him that you look at him in a certain way so he feels loved.

Because you are both so visual, you both may be caught up in a whirl of looking good. It might be hard for you to change gears and deal with emotional trauma or to understand a hysterical teenager or depressed friend.

Visual Woman/Auditory Man

He hardly ever measures up to your visual standards in how he dresses. You will probably spend your whole life picking lint off him and making sure his colors match when he goes out. On the other hand, you can have everything exactly the way you want it visually because he really doesn't care enough to do any decorating on his own. Nor does he have a clear picture of what he wants. He'll appreciate what you do to make his surroundings pleasant because he knows he couldn't do it himself.

It'll be frustrating for you when he forgets to look at the list you've made or to put things back where they belong. You can train him to remember where things were, but it takes lots of patience.

Although he sometimes doesn't seem to notice, he does admire you and the way you are able to arrange things to look right. He knows that if it weren't for you, he'd never be able to find anything. Try to remember that he doesn't process information visually the way you do. Don't write things down, tell him.

You can stimulate him visually by combining auditory and visual stimulation. Instead of taking him to an art gallery, take him to an art auction where there is constant verbal as well as visual stimulation. Hearing about art is just as important to him as seeing it. Don't just show him something, talk to him about it.

You may be tempted to assume he can see how much you care about him because of the way you look at him or because of the cute notes and loving cards you send. Unfortunately he needs to hear the words, not just see signs of your love. No matter how you decorate, diet, dress or look lovingly, don't forget to tell him your feelings as well.

Visual Woman/Feelings Man

Your feelings man may seem like an enigma to you. He's so . . . well, sloppy, and yet he's so lovable. You sometimes don't understand how you fell for a guy who looks like he does, who seems not to notice anything, and who can't match his socks. But then he "reads" your mood, puts his arms around you, and you completely forget the worn-out jeans and old T-shirts he loves to wear.

You'll have trouble getting your feelings man to do something that seems visually obvious to you—unless you remember how he is motivated. If the plan is to make him or something else look better, he'll drag his feet.

When you want to redecorate, don't expect him to help or be the least bit enthusiastic. He doesn't want to be disturbed. If the paint is cracking off the ceiling, he doesn't care. If the stuffing is coming out of the couch, he doesn't want a new one. He's comfortable with the existing mess. He gets attached to a routine easily and any threat that he'll have to change it will get him upset.

You can make changes, but it'll be hard to get him to agree ahead of time. Once the old sofa's gone and he's happily entrenched in a new (comfortable) one, he'll probably be glad you made the change, but not before.

Some women with feelings men don't tell them ahead of time when they're going to make changes around the house. They know he'll be upset. The new couch, the new rugs, the new appliances just appear. Sometimes he doesn't even notice. When he does, he's always sad for a moment because he was very attached to the old stuff.

You can stimulate him visually by first starting in his feelings Love Language and then switching to visual. Instead of taking him to an art exhibit of paintings, take him to an art "experience" or an exhibit of sculpture, where he can be part of the art or touch it. Offer him new physical sensations combined with visual ones. Take him to an erotic art exhibit. Touch him a lot.

Don't think you can pull the wool over his eyes and dazzle him with fast footwork. He may seem slow but his intuition will tell him you're up to something. He'll know if you're hiding something behind a pretty façade.

Actually, that's the best part of being with a feelings man. He can sense your feelings, so you might as well relax and just be yourself. He loves you when you get up in the morning, no matter how awful you look. He loves you if you're fat or out of shape or sick or sad. He's the most nurturing of men, always quick with a hug or a kiss, sensitive and understanding. Once you have a feelings man's love, you have it forever.

7

The Auditory Woman

YOU'RE the one everybody listens to, the advice giver, the good communicator. You are reasonable and rational, a good friend and helpful arbitrator. You can hear both sides of a question without prejudice. Your advice is well thought out and friends often come to you with their problems.

You are almost always calm and rational, and your ideas are both creative and practical. You talk on the phone a lot. If you don't have a long in-depth conversation every so often, you feel deprived. You are capable of sharing a great deal verbally, sometimes more than others want to hear.

Your idea of intimacy is a good conversation, even over the telephone. You prefer talking on the phone to writing a letter. You can hear things in people's voices and in what they say that others can't. You are sensitive to every pronoun, alert to every inflection. A simple "Hello" can say more to you than to others. You can read people by the tone in their voices.

Friends report entire conversations to you for analysis or advice, and you can almost hear them as if they were actually happening. You are capable of creating whole scripts in your mind, hearing entire conversations.

You are a good public speaker. With your vivid imagination, you are a fabulous storyteller. You have a pleasant voice and the ability to charm people over the phone. You are able to convince people of just about anything and make a terrific saleswoman.

One of my very auditory friends is the sales director for a large medical instruments firm. In her job, she has to convince busy doctors and hospital staffs to buy expensive new devices and learn to use them. Her sales are always at the top of the company rankings because she has the ability to determine exactly what a prospective customer wants to hear and she is able to say it in exactly the right way. Doctors love the sound of her voice and the way she has of explaining the new instruments to them. She is frequently flown around the country by her company to visit hospitals and teach how to use the instruments. Her ability to understand people's problems and confusion makes her a perfect saleswoman and trainer.

Since I am auditory, I love to go on radio and TV shows and talk about my books. People often ask if I don't get tired of answering the same questions over and over again. Of course not. As a typical auditory person, I love to talk. In the past year, I was frequently asked to give speeches. At first, I was concerned about getting up in front of a large group and just talking for an hour or more, but it was amazing how quickly I began to enjoy speaking to large groups and even getting paid to speak.

One time, I had just made a speech at the Woman's Faire in downtown Los Angeles and was rushing to give a three-hour seminar about thirty miles away. Halfway to the seminar I realized I had forgotten my notes. I panicked, but it turned out to be one of my best seminars ever. However, it ran for more than four hours because I had talked too much. I discovered I needed my notes more to limit what I had to say than to make sure I had enough to last.

The problem with being an auditory woman is that you will be prone to creating scenarios in your head. Little voices will tell you all sorts of horrible things that could happen and you could get bogged down by them. One auditory woman was always hearing a little voice that said she was too ugly to be loved and her husband was going to leave her. I could really sympathize with her. When I first met my husband, Marshall, I was taunted by little voices predicting a relationship catastrophe of some kind like the ones I'd had in the past. After becoming impatient with sophisticated psychological theories about what caused the voices, I found that there is a simple solution: Just tell the little voices to shut up. It works.

Auditory Woman/Visual Man

If you are an auditory woman in love with a visual man, you will have to learn to talk his visual language. You will also have to learn to become visually aware so that you can keep your visual man happy.

I'm an auditory woman married to a very visual man. When Marshall moved in, my kitchen looked like something out of a Cathy cartoon, and the back yard was a jungle. Marshall, naturally, likes things looking neat and orderly. We could have had real problems, but fortunately I got Marshall involved in my research on Love Languages. After we understood our differences, we were able to work things out.

First, we agreed that he would have certain areas in the house which were his to arrange; I would have other areas which were mine to get as disorganized as I wished; the remaining areas we compromised on. When Marshall felt an overwhelming urge to clear out the back yard, he explained to me that the dogs would be quieter out in the yard and then cleared it to please his visual sense. When our old, mono television was about to drive me up the wall, I decided the time had come for a new stereo set. So I reminded Marshall of how much better the room would look with a component system that could be hidden away when not in use. He agreed in a flash.

Just remember, instead of talking about how things sound, talk to your visual man about how things look. Tell him the sink would look more shipshape if the faucet didn't drip. Then he may fix it. Don't even waste your breath telling him the dripping noise is driving you nuts.

Pay special attention to his little visual arrangements, such as how he lines up his toiletries, and try not to mix them up. His arrangements of things may not be important to you, but they are to him.

When you talk to him, make sure he *sees* what you're talking about. Don't just tell him things, describe what you're talking about in visual terms. Make a special effort to think in pictures. Use "show and tell." He needs to see things as well as hearing about them. If you tell him about your day and he's not listening, it's probably because he's not getting the picture.

Or you may be telling him about how you feel, in which case you may be a feelings woman (see chapter 8).

Auditory Woman/Auditory Man

You will both be happy listening and talking to each other. With auditory couples, the biggest problem is not a lack of conversation, it's who's going to talk and who's going to listen.

Your auditory man will always put what you say and exactly the way you say it ahead of everything. He loves the sound of your voice, that's why he hangs around, but be sure to keep it pleasant sounding. You'll be able to convince him to do just about anything if you remember that what he really loves is a pleasant, happy sound in your voice. So who likes an unpleasant, disagreeable sound? Well, some people won't notice as much as he will.

You know instinctively which sounds annoy him, like crashing dishes, dripping faucets and screechy friends. You and he should have no problem agreeing on a house in a quiet neighborhood, for example. Together, you could possibly miss a lot, though, because neither of you is likely to notice something visual, like the roof falling in—at least not until you hear the crash.

You are both happiest at small intimate gatherings where everyone can talk.

You and your auditory mate will keep each other happy because he will understand your need to hear certain words, perhaps "I love you" or some pet phrase, over and over. You will understand that he also needs to hear certain words said by you in order to feel really loved. By learning to say the right words to each other, you will both be happy for a long time.

Don't forget, though, you and he may have different auditory scenarios worked out. You thought he was going to say a certain thing, or that he should have said it—perhaps an apology made in a certain way. He may not always say exactly what you hoped he'd say in the way you wanted him to say it. But then, you won't always say exactly what he was hoping either.

✳ *Auditory Woman/Feelings Man*

You and your feelings man are made for each other. He will be sensitive and overflowing with emotions and you will be able to help provide the words for how he feels. When you are overflowing with words and talking about how you feel, he will be the one to take you in his arms and hug away your problems.

If you talk to him on some abstract level, he may tune out, but you can talk and talk about how you feel and he'll always be a ready and willing listener. He'll understand if Bach soothes your soul and the Boomtown Rats move you to dance. He'll respect your need for quiet and solitude and he'll be happy to let you talk for him. He admires your eloquence and will do whatever it takes to keep you happy. All you have to do is tell him what you want.

On the other hand, he can be easily hurt by words you think are cute or funny or clever. Be careful that your ability to turn a phrase doesn't make him feel like the butt of a joke.

Be sure to touch him a lot. Just telling him you love him isn't enough. He needs to be touched to feel loved, while you only need to hear the right words said in the right way.

Because he's a feelings man, he'll sometimes surprise you by knowing how you feel before you've told him. He can sense when you're upset and trying to cover things up with a lot of fast talk.

Your feelings man is a homebody. He loves to be comfortable. Don't expect him to match your energy level. He'd rather just sit still and mellow out. If you try to dress him up and drag him out when he wants to be home, he'll just be miserable and ruin your good time too.

To you, he may seem to love blindly without any reason, or to take a dislike to someone with no apparent cause. You may find him frustrating when he won't give you a logical reason for the way he behaves or the decisions he makes. Remember, though, often he can't give you a logical explanation because there is none. He feels the way he does and that's it. A special intuitive sixth sense drives him, a sense that's beyond logical explanation. Actually, you two make a good team, with your logic and his sixth sense.

8

The Feelings Woman

YOU'RE the caretaker, the person people turn to for warmth and understanding. People come to you with their deepest secrets, their innermost confessions, and their most farfetched dreams and schemes, because you're so sympathetic, so nonjudgmental.

You're sympathetic to everyone because you can sense their pain. You understand both sides of a question because you can relate to how everyone feels. You have lots of friends, and they sometimes just want to be around you because you seem to radiate warmth and nurturing.

You are sometimes too sensitive for your own good. Because you relate so well to everyone, people sometimes take advantage of you. You are known as a softie, an easy touch, always there and ready to give. Often you give more than others really deserve, they give little or nothing back, and you wind up feeling cheated and unappreciated.

You are easily hurt, and because you are so kind, you often won't tell the person who hurt you how you feel. Your understanding of others makes it difficult for you to get angry at them. You are more likely to find excuses for the ones you love than to blame them for anything.

You make the important decisions in your life based on

how you feel. Sometimes you will overlook the facts completely and rely solely on how you feel about something. But you are very intuitive; the "vibes" you get in a situation usually lead to the right conclusion.

You are slow to anger and quick to forgive. When you love, you give your all, sometimes blindly neglecting yourself for others.

As a feelings woman, you are likely to be in one of the nurturing professions like psychology, teaching or nursing. You really like people and enjoy being with them.

Men are automatically drawn to you because of your easy acceptance of them just the way they are, with all their foibles and eccentricities.

When friends come to you in pain, you intuitively know exactly the right words to say to make them feel better. My feelings friend is the one I turn to when anything goes wrong. She always has a kind word to say, encouragement, and a warm hug. If I'm exasperated with my work, she tells me how much better I'm doing. If I'm late with an article, she tells me how much later other people have been. If I'm impatient with my husband, she tells me how much worse her ex was than any man I've ever known.

My feelings friend can take the most annoying day and make it happy again. She's the one I call when I just have to have a cheery afternoon lunch or tea or shopping expedition. She is ever happy for me when I am happy, sad when I'm sad.

Her house is bright and comfortable more than chic. Her look is more earth mother than beauty queen, and yet she radiates an inner beauty that many beauty queens lack. And can she cook! A meal at her house is an occasion, a time for friends to gather and eat in relaxed informality. It may not be the most picture-perfect meal you've ever seen, but the taste is out of this world, and there's always lots for seconds and even thirds. Her fridge is never empty of fabulous leftovers.

Her wardrobe is mostly comfortable cottons with draw-strings and shapeless sweats. She's built more for comfort than for speed and would rather spend the day cooking and gardening than going to an art show or a concert. Her calm descends over and quells almost any storm, and her love seems to spread over everyone with whom she comes in contact.

Feelings Woman/Visual Man

If you're a feelings woman in love with a visual man, you will have to learn to appeal to his visual perspective.

When he walks in the door at night, a warm hug and a kiss are nice, but he wants to get a good look at you first. He likes visual words as well. Instead of talking to him about how you feel, talk to him about how you see things. Instead of trying to communicate your feelings to him nonverbally, which probably won't work, think about ways to show him your love. Give him flowers, write him love notes, frame a picture of you looking at him lovingly and put it where he can see it often. Don't just depend on him feeling your love unless he can see it as well.

Find out exactly what your visual man likes to see you wear and wear it for him. Find out the expressions he likes to see on your face and look at him that way. Consult him about decorating, his favorite colors, and how he'd like the furniture arranged. Let him know that you like the way he looks; it's important to him.

Don't worry about cooking exciting, delicious gourmet meals for him unless you're willing to go all the way and make them look good. You're likely to stop before you put the parsley on the plate, but your visual man needs the parsley in order to enjoy the taste.

Don't waste your breath telling him how bad you feel going to a party in last year's dress. Tell him you have to have a new dress because the old one doesn't look right for the occasion. He'll be much more sympathetic.

If you have little things that mean a lot to you—mementos of trips you've taken together, the stuffed dolls you've saved from college—don't expect him to appreciate their value, especially if they're not really attractive. Don't put them anywhere he might find them, because he loves to throw out old stuff. He'd rather have lots of clean space in the garage than see it cluttered with keepsakes. So hide that first corsage he gave you or he'll throw it away as dead flowers. Put the wedding matches you saved in a special place or he's sure to use them to light the barbeque. Your heart will be broken and he'll never understand why.

I have a good friend who is a feelings woman married to a visual man. For years, she complained about how cold he was, how unromantic. Even after being reminded, he often forgot her birthday and their anniversary. Finally, she tried a new technique. She wrote each anniversary, each birthday, every holiday in his daily calendar. Then two weeks before the date she put a reminder in blue ink. One week before, the reminder was in red. Guess what? Just switching from reminding him vocally to reminding him with something he could see did the trick. He never forgot again.

Feelings Woman/Auditory Man

You can get along well with the auditory man because you are both primarily interested in good vibes. You like to keep a happy house; he likes a house filled with pleasant sounds. You can both be happy together.

However, because you intuitively sense when everything's okay, you might expect him to. Don't. Also, don't expect him to feel loved automatically because it's in his heart or in yours. Your auditory man needs more reassurance of your love than your adoring look or even a special hug or kiss or great sex. He likes all those things, but he needs more. He needs you to tell him over and over again how much you love him. No matter how many times you say "I love you," he never gets tired of hearing the words.

Because it's important to you that your mate be happy, you

can become upset by your auditory man's moods. He's the kind of guy who can have a whole conversation in his head and then get upset by it. Remember that you are not responsible for his moods. He is. If he seems upset, ask him to tell you about it. Since he's basically very communicative and you are basically understanding and supportive, he will tell you all about his feelings and all will be well.

Since you are so sensitive, you will sometimes feel as if he is insensitive to your feelings. He isn't. He just can't help saying whatever he thinks.

If your best meal leaves him cold, if your back rubs and kisses haven't gotten him in the mood, if your satin sheets haven't turned him on, think about the sounds of love. Play his favorite music, talk dirty to him, whisper sweet nothings in his ear. No matter how much you love him or lust after him, he'll never get the message unless he hears it.

Feelings Woman/Feelings Man

A feelings man brings out the best in a feelings woman. He appreciates your sensitivity and feels secure in your warmth. You two understand each other on a deep, spiritual level. You both know you were meant for each other. He touches you the way you always wanted to be touched. His eyes reach into your soul and you read each other's emotions without a word.

He loves the way you cry at movies and when you're really happy. You love the way he cries at movies and on sentimental occasions. The two of you are so sensitive that you can be in danger of total withdrawal from the harsh, cruel world. You're really happiest at home together.

You both are most comfortable in old clothes and your home is warm and comfortable, just the way he likes it. He loves the soft fabrics you choose and the easy way you have of over-looking flaws. You make the best of whatever is and he feels loved for himself, and secure.

You communicate more with a touch, the squeeze of a

hand, or a soft kiss than any words can say. You love long silences when the two of you just sit together and hug.

Because you both tend to go with your feelings, sometimes you may be in danger of getting ripped off by unscrupulous salesmen or scheming business associates. Your feelings are easily hurt and you feel betrayed when you trust someone and they abuse that trust. So check people out, and be extra careful to get things in writing, even if you do feel good vibes about a person. Let people know you're not pushovers or easy marks just because you're both warm and friendly.

Be sure to take time to do something wonderful just for yourself once in a while. You could be in danger of forgetting yourself and spending all your time making sure he's feeling good and he's happy. Of course, when you're both happy, your day is full of joy, you don't have a problem in the world.

9

Love Language
Self-Test

IF you've read the previous chapters on Love Languages and still have questions about your Love Language or your mate's, this test will help you decide whether you and your mate are visual, auditory or feelings-oriented.

1. Given $1,000 to spend on one of the following, which would you choose?
a) A new mattress
b) A new stereo
c) A new television
Me_____ Him_____

2. Which would you rather do?
a) Stay home and eat a home-cooked meal
b) Go out to a concert
c) Go to a movie
Me_____ Him_____

3. Given a choice of activities at a resort, which would you choose?
a) Going to a lecture
b) Exploring hiking trails
c) Relaxing and doing nothing
Me_____ Him_____

4. Which of these rooms would you most enjoy?
a) One with a terrific view
b) One with an ocean breeze
c) One in a quiet corner
Me_____ Him_____

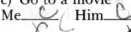

5. To which event would you rather go?
a) A wedding
b) An art exhibit
c) A cocktail party
Me_____ Him_____

6. Which are you considered?
a) Athletic
b) Intellectual
c) Humanitarian
Me_____ Him_____

7. How do you most often keep in touch?
a) By talking on the phone.
b) By writing letters
c) By having lunch
Me_____ Him_____

8. How do you prefer to spend time?
a) Talking
b) Touching
c) Looking
Me_____ Him_____

9. If you lost your keys, what would you do?
a) Look for them
b) Shake your pocketbook or pockets to hear them jingle
c) Feel around for them
Me_____ Him_____

10. If you were going to be stranded on a desert island, what would you most want to take along?
a) Some good books
b) A portable radio
c) Your sleeping bag
Me_____ Him_____

11. Which type of dresser are you?
a) Immaculate
b) Casual
c) Very casual
Me_____ Him_____

12. Which of these would you rather be?
a) In the know
b) Very chic
c) Comfortable
Me_____ Him_____

13. If you had unlimited money, what would you do?
a) Buy a great house and stay there
b) Travel and see the world
c) Join in the social scene
Me_____ Him_____

14. If you could, which would you rather be?
a) A great doctor
b) A great musician
c) A great painter
Me_____ Him_____

15. Which do you think is sexier?
a) Soft lighting
b) Perfume
c) Special music
Me_____ Him_____

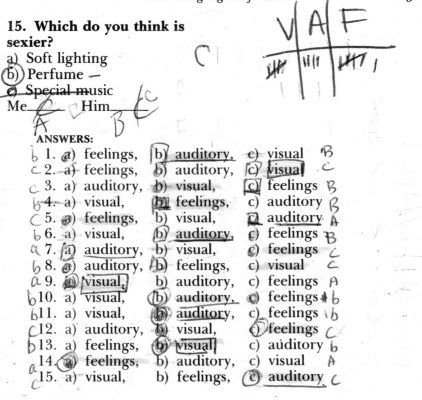

ANSWERS:

1. a) feelings, b) auditory, c) visual
2. a) feelings, b) auditory, c) visual
3. a) auditory, b) visual, c) feelings
4. a) visual, b) feelings, c) auditory
5. a) feelings, b) visual, c) auditory
6. a) visual, b) auditory, c) feelings
7. a) auditory, b) visual, c) feelings
8. a) auditory, b) feelings, c) visual
9. a) visual, b) auditory, c) feelings
10. a) visual, b) auditory, c) feelings
11. a) visual, b) auditory, c) feelings
12. a) auditory, b) visual, c) feelings
13. a) feelings, b) visual, c) auditory
14. a) feelings, b) auditory, c) visual
15. a) visual, b) feelings, c) auditory

Count the number of visual, auditory and feelings preferences for both you and your mate. You will quickly be able to see your primary, secondary and terciary choices. Where you have the most answers will be an indication of your primary Love Language, the next will be your secondary, the third, your least active Love Language.

Me: Visual_____ Auditory_____; Visual_____

Him: Visual_____; Auditory_____ Visual_____

10

Mirroring

WATCH people who are in love. You will notice something interesting. They seem to look alike, sit alike, dress alike, even sound alike. They are naturally in tune with each other, totally and absolutely in sync. They somehow seem to belong together. The longer people are together, the more alike they become.

You see them in church, you see them at the supermarket, you see them everywhere—couples wearing the same colors, walking with the same gait. They even have similar nervous habits. If he jiggles his foot, watch her move hers, or tap her fingers, in exactly the same rhythm.

Listen to them finish each other's sentences, or watch how when one talks, the other nods, as if in silent agreement. Listen to the words they use, their accents, the rate at which they speak. Notice how similar they sound.

Look at their shoulders go up and down as they seem to breathe in unison.

Notice how he changes his position in a chair to match hers. She puts her hand on her chin, he does the same. Watch how easily and naturally they seem to fit together.

Being psychically "in tune" makes these couples act alike without ever consciously thinking about it. They have developed a deep psychological rapport. The opposite is true as well. You can easily tell if a couple is having relationship trouble, because they will be out of sync. Watch them together.

If she sits forward in the chair, does he? Or does he sit back? Does he cross his legs, followed by her uncrossing hers? Is he relaxed, with his hands behind his head, while she is nervous and fidgety? Do they sit close, or apart?

By observing just how dissimilar a couple is acting, you can often tell they're having problems before they know it themselves.

Being deeply in love means being "in tune" with your mate, and when you are in tune, you tend to act the same—you "mirror" each other. That's common observation. The fascinating secret to mirroring is that this process works in reverse. If you mirror your mate, you will get more in tune with him, which will enhance and deepen your love.

How does this process work? Why does it work? It all has to do with trust and comfort levels.

Creating a Comfort Level

Trust is the prime ingredient of love. Before we can love someone, we need to trust them totally. We need to feel that we can let our guard down, be vulnerable without the other person taking advantage of us.

Where does trust come from? Theoretically, you could build that kind of total trust, step by step, with anyone. But we *automatically* tend to trust other people when they are like us. It's human nature.

We tend to be fearful of what we don't know, and comfortable with what we do know. Each of us is most comfortable with our personal identity. Since we all like comfort, we prefer being with people who look like us, dress like us and, unfortunately, whose skin is the same color and whose accents are familiar. That's why there is so much prejudice in the world. We have trouble trusting people who seem different.

Think about your relationship, the times when you've felt most in love. At those times, didn't you and your mate also feel most in tune with each other? Your comfort level, your sense of total trust of each other was at a peak.

The ultimate in mirroring occurs right after you've made love. Have you ever noticed that as you're lying together, perhaps both of you lying on your sides, his front curved against your back, breathing together, you feel an amazing closeness, a feeling of oneness? That's because you are mirroring each other's body posture, breathing and mental state. It's just as simple as that.

You don't have to wait helplessly for this comfort level to somehow return to your relationship. Whenever you feel the love or intimacy of your relationship is slipping to one degree or another, mirroring your loved one can bring you back together. Mirroring will re-create that peak of comfort level, that sense of total trust.

And it's so easy! Mirroring simply means sitting, dressing, acting, talking, reflecting another person's behavior.

Now I can already hear some of you asking, "Why should we have to change ourselves for him? Why doesn't he do the mirroring?"

The truth is that men are just not as flexible as women. Try to get him to give up his old slippers or the jacket he's had since college. Try to get him to be nice to someone he doesn't like. See how flexible he is about moving his favorite chair to a different part of the room, or redecorating in a new color scheme, or even sitting on the other end of the sofa.

Men like everything to stay the same. They are more likely to have set routines and want to stick with them. Try changing his dinner hour, or even switching brands of toothpaste. He'll think it's a personal assault. So you may want to think of mirroring as a technique we women can use more adeptly than men, just because we're more flexible.

Also, mirroring is not a loss of self. It is nothing more than you would do for a woman friend. The same woman who is insulted at the suggestion that she mirror her husband would quite naturally ask a girl friend what she was wearing if they are going out together.

Who hasn't had the experience of showing up in a dress and having everyone else show up in jeans? Let a good friend say she's wearing a long dress, and you will too. So what's the big deal about doing it for the man you love to improve your relationship?

Subliminal Power

Instead of worrying about mirroring as a loss of self, understand that it is a way to gain subliminal power, a way of protecting your relationship without having to iron polyester shirts—unless you want to. See it as a way of positively influencing your loved one to love you back.

Power in marriage is a tricky thing today. Many women are upset because they feel they don't have as much power as their husbands. Some women feel it's a matter of money. They think that if they make as much, even more money than the man in their lives, then they will have power in their relationship—but that's just not necessarily true. I've been told by women, "He makes all the money so he says how it can be spent." And I've been told, "We both make about the same amount of money, but I have to do all the housework. He acts like he's more important." And I've even been told, "I make more money than he does, and yet I feel as if he's still the boss."

In each of these instances these women have felt as if the power in their relationships were out of balance. The truth is that even the most successful women often feel as if their husbands or lovers have more power in the relationship than they do—that things are never quite equal. "He feels like he's more important just because he's tall and strong," a highly respected company president told me about her husband.

Men, having always felt as if they had more power in their

relationships, get upset and can become very defensive when their wives begin to change the power balance in the relationship in an obvious way. For instance, she begins to make more money than he does, or she gets an advanced degree, or she is elected president of their church group. In each of these instances, husbands have been upset and difficult because they've felt a loss of power.

Mirroring is a way to gain power without his noticing or getting upset. It's subtle, it's subliminal and it's very, very effective. Once you learn to mirror the man you love, you can get him to do many things he wouldn't have considered before. You can also keep him calm and happy if it happens that the fiscal balance of power is shifting in your direction.

You can even get him to change his mood when he's being difficult, or to become loving when he's acting unlovable. With mirroring, you can suddenly and radically improve his comfort level, and you get your loving mate back.

Conscious Harmony

As long as life is harmonious, all is well, but when it's not, you can consciously bring harmony back into your relationship with mirroring. Suppose the man in your life walks in the door and slumps in a chair, exhausted from a busy day's work? You on the other hand, have just had a shower and are all refreshed, cheery, and bright.

You bustle around, bringing him a cool drink, cooking dinner, plumping pillows. He gets grumpier and grumpier. The worse he gets, the more you bustle around, trying to cheer him up. You suggest, "How about a nice shower?" or "Maybe you'd like to go out to a movie?"

He doesn't want a shower. He doesn't want to be bothered. He sinks deeper and deeper into his foul mood.

Instead of bustling around, trying to convince him that he's not as tired as he thinks he is, or that everything is really just fine with the world, try creating conscious harmony through mirroring. It's a lot easier.

Flop down. Relax. Actually mirror his rotten attitude. But sympathize. Tell him by your movements that you feel the same way he does. The first thing that will happen is you will suddenly be in tune with each other. That alone will make him start to feel better, less isolated and alone. Then you can gradually pull him out of it, perhaps salvaging the whole evening with an investment of fifteen minutes.

Why does it work?

When you look and act differently from the man in your life, he gets the message unconsciously that you don't like the way he is, or that you don't agree with him. Nobody likes to be disagreed with, so he just gets grumpier. But when he sees you matching him, he will feel validated, and he will feel subliminal warmth and comfort. He will want to stay close to you because you are the source of that warmth and comfort.

Mirroring is the simplest method to get someone comfortable with you really quickly. You can use it to develop rapport with your in-laws. You can use it to get your kids to listen. You can use it in meetings and at your job, but best of all, you can use this easy technique to build intimacy and closeness with the man you love.

An amazing thing happens when you begin to mirror the man in your life. He in turn begins to mirror you. In order to be in the lead whenever you want, you'll need to know all the different ways of mirroring so you can vary your strategy and be more effective.

Physical Mirroring

Physical mirroring is like a body language game. If he is slumping, you slump a little. Stand in more or less the same posture he does, cross your leg if he crosses his, lean forward if he leans forward, clasp your hands if he does. If he is cupping his chin in his hand, you rest your chin on yours.

But this is not a game of Monkey See, Monkey Do. It has to be done casually. You don't want him to know what you're doing. Don't be obvious. Make your movements smooth and natural. Don't instantly change position when he does. For example, he moves forward in his chair. You wait several seconds to a minute and then do the same.

And you don't have to mirror him exactly. Say he crosses one leg and begins to jiggle his foot. You wait a few seconds to cross your legs and then notice that if you begin to jiggle your foot too, you will kick each other. So you do something else. You tap your finger instead. Keep your movements smooth and off-hand. Act as though you were unconsciously drawn to sit like him.

Mirroring starts with observing his body language, which is not a bad idea. Body language is more honest than the words people use. Body language rarely lies.

You can tell more about what your man's thinking by watching his body language and facial expressions than by doing anything else. For example, you suggest going out to dinner and a movie. He crosses his arms in front of his chest and says, "Sure, honey, that's fine." You can be certain he doesn't really mean what he says.

Because we all have more conscious control over the words we say than our body language, always believe the body language if the words and body language conflict. The way he stands, whether he follows your body language or not, even his eye movements, will always tell you more than what he says. A woman who learns to really read her man's body language will have the key to the inner man, because his body language will never lie.

Mirror your mate's body language to get in tune with him, but be careful about what you mirror—you may not want to get permanently in tune with everything about him. Don't mirror something like cuticle picking, nail biting or hair pulling, for example, unless you are prepared to deal with learning a new bad habit.

When I met my husband, I mirrored his habit of picking his cuticles. We were really in tune. Soon, I had an adoring husband, but I also had the messiest cuticles you've ever seen. I am still working on breaking myself of the habit.

Over the past years, I have used mirroring in many other situations besides just love. I have mirrored editors, by reflecting the tone of their voice on the phone or the accent they have, to increase their comfort level with me and improve our communication.

I have mirrored talk-show hosts like Phil Donahue and Merv Griffin. Getting quickly into rapport with them helped me get relaxed, made for a better interview, and got us what we were both working for—a good show.

I have mirrored reporters both in the United States and Europe while they were interviewing me, and I always got more space in print than they had originally intended, because we established rapport and found we had a lot in common.

I have mirrored clients who've come to me for help so that they would relax and it would be easier to help them. The mirroring made them trust me, and then they quickly revealed their innermost problems and feelings.

I have mirrored people I was interviewing for magazine articles and found that they told me more revealing and intimate information than they would have otherwise.

I have mirrored judges and lawyers while testifying as an expert witness on relationships, and I have mirrored many couples, both men and women, while interviewing them for this book. Never has anyone said, "How come you're sitting like me?" or "Why do you sound like me?"

The trickiest mirroring incident I remember was when I was being interviewed by a reporter for the *Los Angeles Times*. He had already been to my seminar and this was a follow-up interview to make sure he had everything right for his article. I wanted to mirror him, but I didn't want to be obvious. After all, I had just taught him how to mirror, so I suspected he might catch me at it.

Also, I told him how I had brazenly mirrored my husband by dressing like him when we were dating, so I didn't dare try dressing like the reporter. Besides, there was going to be a photographer there to take a picture. I definitely didn't want my picture in the *Times* with me dressed like a reporter. I was very nervous and wanted to make sure he would write a good story in my hometown newspaper.

What I did was very subtle. I petted my dog in the exact same rhythm he was breathing. As he breathed in, I stroked her back, as he breathed out, I stroked again.

Guess what? The story was so nice, I couldn't have written it better myself. Even my mother loved it.

And he even mentioned me stroking ". . . a sleek Doberman with the improbable name of Precious." His subconscious noticed something about the dog petting, but he never knew it was in the exact rhythm of his breathing.

You may think, Sure, maybe Tracy can say that no one has ever caught her mirroring, but what if I'm not that subtle? And my husband knows me like a book. If I suddenly start sitting like him, and standing the way he does, or moving like him, he's going to know. . . . But he won't. First of all, you *can* learn to be subtle and unobvious. Second, if he does notice, his reaction will not be what you're thinking.

What if your mate notices that you are sitting like he is, then changing your posture soon after he does? He will simply assume that he is so dominant and so fascinating to you that he is leading you, and you are following him without your even being aware of it. And the more he thinks about it, the better off you are. When he thinks about how he is able to affect you, he is overcome with his own attractiveness. He loves the attention and feels virile and sexy. There is no greater allure for any man than to think he is impressing you.

But mirroring is not just following his lead and impressing him with that. Once you're in sync with your man, *you're* in a position to lead.

Leading Him

Mirroring merely gets you in sync with your mate. As soon as you are, you have gained a tremendous personal power, because now you can begin to change the tune.

All the greatest salesmen in the world know about mirroring. They are masters at it, because they know they can never make a sale unless they first get in tune with the prospect. A book salesman I know actually changes his accent for whatever area he's selling in—he sounds Bostonian in Boston, like a Philadelphian in Philadelphia, like a southerner in Atlanta, and like a good 'ole boy in Texas.

Great attorneys like Melvin Belli, who convince juries to award millions of dollars to people, are experts in mirroring. Heads of state and heads of corporations are skilled at reflecting as a technique to establish rapport under the most difficult of circumstances.

Mirroring can help you, too, when your man is difficult and balky. Let's say he's being very negative about something, sitting on the sofa with his arms crossed. Now we've all heard that when people cross their arms in front of them, or cross their legs, it's a sign that they want to put distance between you and them. But if your man crosses his arms in front of himself, you do it too. Before you can lead him out of his snit, you must mirror him to get totally in sync with him.

So cross your arms if his are crossed. Mirror his other body language, talk to him in his Love Language and check his eyes to see if you're getting through—then uncross your arms. If he follows and uncrosses his arms, then you know you are leading him. If he doesn't uncross his arms, you can cross yours again and start the process over. When he follows your movement, you will know you are getting him into a state of agreement with you, without his ever having said a word.

Use mirroring to get what you want in your relationship—more romance, better sex, dinner out, more time together, or just to make sure you have his attention.

How many times have I heard women complain, "He never listens to me." One easy solution is simply to mirror him when you talk to him. Don't tell him something really important while you're reading a magazine or chopping onions. Stop what you're doing and get in tune with him. Mirror him for just a couple of minutes, make small talk about something until you're sure you're in tune with him, then talk about what's important to you.

He'll pay attention in a way he didn't before. Just by giving him your full attention, he will feel that what you have to say is important. Subconsciously, he'll be inclined to agree with you because he feels in sync, and his comfort level will be high.

Dawn, a 33-year-old new mother and former editor, was angry with her husband Glenn, a stockbroker. For two weeks she had been trying to tell him that she wanted to go back to work. Whenever she began talking to him about how she felt, he really didn't listen. "There I'd be, telling him some important development in my hunt for a job, and he wouldn't even listen. He'd nod and he'd grunt, but I could tell he didn't hear a word I was saying."

Then Dawn tried mirroring him first. Before getting into what she wanted to talk to him about, she got in sync with him. If she couldn't, because he was hypnotized in front of his stock reports, she waited until she could, usually when he was sitting on the couch reading the paper. Dawn then would first sit beside him, touching him just a little so he knew she was there. After just a couple of minutes of sitting like him, breathing like him, maybe even reading the paper, she'd say, "Glenn, I'd like to talk to you if you could interrupt your reading for a minute. . . ." Since Glenn is auditory, he'd put down the paper and really listen, even if it wasn't a subject he wanted to talk about. When Dawn tried mirroring, Glenn suddenly began to pay attention.

Mirroring has another important benefit, besides getting your man's attention. It allows you to forget about yourself for just a few minutes and really concentrate on him. When you are mirroring him, you don't have to worry about what you're going to say next. You can really listen and get on his wavelength.

When you can get totally in sync with your man you never have to worry about a lack of communication. You'll always be able to reconnect when things go haywire—which they often do in life and in relationships. You will have a way of reaching him no matter how his state of mind may change, whether he's depressed or elated. You'll know how to stay close and create intimacy.

Creating Intimacy

Many people think that intimacy is a given in marriage, that it just comes with the territory. But it's not. Intimacy can only be maintained by paying attention to it, by knowing how much you have and being sensitive to changes in it.

There is nothing wrong with creating intimacy. A created intimacy feels just as good as a "natural" intimacy that just happens when you're both relaxed. In a relationship, the more intimacy, the better. Mirroring is one of the best ways to create intimacy.

When I was interviewing couples about how they had kept their love alive, I remember asking lots of couples, married ten years or so, "What do you do to keep your mate in love?" And many of them didn't know. Or worse yet, didn't do anything.

One couple actually glared at each other and said, "Nothing lately. We haven't done anything at all for the last few years." And then they began to growl at each other about why they didn't do anything and who should. Undaunted, I interrupted the battle and asked, "Well, what did you used to do?"

Since I expected another "I don't know," I was really surprised to hear that they used to do lots of things they don't do anymore. They somehow had slipped into mirroring each other's habit of doing nothing. And who knows who was the first one to do nothing? But one of them had to break the pattern or their relationship would continue to get worse.

After the interview, I talked to the wife and suggested mirroring as a technique for her to use to renew intimacy. Later, she called me, excited, to say, "Not only did the mirroring work whenever I tried it on him, but now I think he's starting to do it to me!"

Keeping Romance Alive

"We had more money then," or "We didn't have kids," or "We weren't working so hard," are the excuses I hear when couples come to me about where the romance has gone. One of the usual real reasons is that they used to mirror each other's romantic habits—and then they stopped, and began to mirror their noncommunicative, unromantic, nonintimate habits.

One way to bring romance back into your life is by doing something romantic for your man. One wife complained to me, "He never brings me flowers." The husband said, "Oh yes, I do. I bring you lots of flowers."

"But he always picks them in the park or steals them over someone's fence. I don't want 'ripped-off roses.' I want him to buy me flowers, like a bouquet from the florist, or even from the grocery store."

Guess what? She had never bought *him* flowers. As a matter of fact, she had never made any romantic gestures toward him. She'd always thought that was the man's part that he had to be intimate first, then she'd react.

She suddenly realized that it was within her power to bring romance to her marriage. After she learned to mirror her husband whenever they were together, she realized that mirroring works both ways. By setting an example of acting romantic herself and bringing him flowers, her husband began to mirror her new romantic attitude, and their marriage was revitalized.

Starting with simple physical mirroring, you can work wonders with your relationship. The immediate effect is that you will be able to influence your man whenever you wish. But there's more. When you establish a comfort level and a rhythm of mirroring and being together, your partner will yearn to come back to you and that comfort zone whenever you are apart.

We all yearn for the familiar and comfortable, also for the release of tension. Because your mate is so relaxed in your presence, you will be the signal for his release of tension. He will not be able to stay away from you for long because you will be the only one who makes him feel perfectly content.

11

Advanced Mirroring

PERHAPS you have felt perfectly in tune with the world, playing with your children in the park or spending a day with a good friend. You and your friend go shopping together and your rhythms are alike. Walking together, you intuitively know when to speed up or slow down. You finish your lunch almost at the same time. You both tire and want to go home after so many hours trying on clothes. You have reached a comfort zone, a sympatico state of unconscious mirroring.

By creating that same rhythm with the man you love, you can be happy and comfortable together forever.

Mirroring Rhythms

Your mate's rhythm is very closely keyed to his primary Love Language. Your visual man has a very speedy rhythm. He has to be on the move all the time because he gets almost all his information and input through his eyes. He is often accused of being hyperactive, a workaholic, having ants in his pants, even of being "on something." But that's just the way he is.

Your auditory or hearing man will move a little slower. He moves around just enough to get into hearing range, since he gets most of his information and processes it that way. Sometimes he seems off in his own little world. Some people even accuse him of being lazy, but he's not. His mind is very busy, even when his body isn't.

The feeling man tends to be slowest moving. He gets his information through his feelings, so all he has to do is sit there and feel. He's often falsely accused of being unmotivated or lazy. He's not. He's busy being in touch with things that most of us miss.

Generally, you can go by your man's primary Love Language to sense his rhythms, but some men switch Love Languages from primary to secondary ones, or they may push themselves into a different state.

You can get your visual man to relax, but first you have to speed up and get in his rhythm. Then you'll be in sync. When you start gradually to slow back down, he'll be drawn to follow you.

When you mirror your mate's rhythm, it's not the exact movement you reproduce, but the beat. Mirroring rhythm is more subtle than physically mirroring body language. In other words, if he's tapping his finger, you could jiggle your foot and be in the same rhythm with him without doing exactly what he's doing.

You can mirror the rhythm of his speech or his favorite music. You can even stroke him in the same rhythm as his very own breathing.

Mirroring Breathing

You can create a wonderful intimacy, where you're warmed by each other's presence, just by mirroring his breathing.

Mirroring his breathing is something you can do anywhere and is an instant way to get totally on his wavelength, especially when you're feeling distant for one reason or another. Just watch his shoulders and you can tell how he's breathing. You are probably already aware of the subtle differences between your breathing pattern and your mate's. Perhaps when you're lying next to him at night, you notice he breathes quicker than you do, or slower.

The faster-breathing person is almost always more visual than the slow breather. On the other hand, the slow breather is sure to be more in touch with his or her feelings.

Breathing in sync with your loved one is not only warm and intimate, it is also very sexy. Subliminally, he'll feel the same sense of safety and trust that a baby feels when it hears its mother's heartbeat.

You can find out a lot about yourself and your mate by breathing together and differently. See if you can get him to change his breathing rhythm to match yours. First, though, you have to breathe like him. Then change slowly and see if he follows. If you are not "out of sync" with him in some other respect, he will invariably follow.

Breathing together can bring you close when you're feeling alienated. It can increase your sexual awareness because a change in the rhythm of his breathing is an indication of his being aroused. Most importantly, breathing together can create the habit of feeling intimate when he's with you, of feeling as if you two are inextricably bound on some deep, unconscious level. It can create a sensation of oneness and belonging together.

You don't have to breathe the way he does all the time, just at those special moments when you want to increase closeness and intimacy.

Mirroring Emotions

Naturally, you can't be expected to feel what your mate feels exactly when he does. Nor can he expect that of you. So, to get in sync, who's going to change their mood or emotion?

As I've said before, *you* are. You have to be flexible—at

least at the beginning—to teach him how to be more responsive. We women have had to get power through our wits, not our brawn. Since men don't change easily by themselves, there is just one way to change a man: by changing yourself. Then he will change in reaction to the changes in you.

You don't really have to get yourself into a totally angry or depressed mood to make your mate feel that you understand his anger or depression. Mirror his body language, of course, and then communicate with him in his Love Language.

Give the visual man a very sympathetic look and say, "I can see why you're angry." For the auditory man, bang something in sympathy and say, "I hear you. I can sure hear why you're angry. Those S.O.B.'s . . ." And give the feelings man an understanding touch and say, "I understand why you're angry. It upsets me, too."

If he is angry or depressed, *don't* try to be bright and cheery. Don't try to play cutesie and tickle him. Just communicate that you are indeed in tune with him, you are affected by how he feels, and you love him. Sympathize. That will get you "in sync."

A very successful saleswoman came to me for advice in handling her husband. They had only been married for a couple of years and there was a definite problem with their relationship. Dick's personality was almost manic, up one minute, down the next. Tricia was exactly the opposite—almost always happy, outgoing and very social.

As with any two-career couple, there were days when Tricia would have a major business success and Dick would have a big disappointment. She would come home elated, and there would be Dick, acting as if his best friend had just died.

"It wouldn't be so bad if he'd just keep his ill-temper and bad mood to himself," Tricia told me, "but he spreads it all over me. He attacks me and snarls about everything until I finally begin to agree with him. And by then, I feel as if it's really true.

"By then he's got me convinced that life is horrible, we'll never live as well as our parents, and we probably should never have married in the first place. I don't know how I let him drag me down the way he does, but I do. And then, it's like somebody threw a switch. The minute he gets me really down, into tears and crying, then he suddenly brightens up like somebody had waved a magic happy wand over his head."

Dick wanted Tricia to be in tune with his bad mood so much that he would do anything he could to get her there. It was a sign that she really loved him, he thought, if she would share his misery.

In some ways, Dick was just acting out something we all think—that if someone loves us, then they're happy if we're happy, sad when we're sad, romantic when we're romantic, worried when we're worried and sexy when we're sexy. Unfortunately, that's not always the case. But if you can try to get in sync with your mate and sympathize enough or at least act like you're happy when he's happy and sad when he's sad, he's going to feel better about your relationship.

Tricia promised she'd try it, and sure enough, the next time Dick was really bummed out over something, she sat down and got right into his mood. She reflected his downtrodden body language, she voiced her opinion on everything being rotten, just the way he said it was. And she did it right away, before he got a chance to feel unloved because she was being happy when he was sad.

"It was really wonderful," she reported back the next week. "Dick actually tried to cheer me up. I was so touched."

Tricia also increased her sales volume by over 20 percent by using the same method with her clients. "Now I get in their mood first, then I sell them the whole store," she laughed.

When you mirror your mate's emotions and really get in tune with him, something you need to know may come out of the deep level of communication you establish with him at that time.

Celine's husband, George, a sometimes-out-of-work freelance news cameraman, was constantly depressed when he didn't have an assignment. "So I try to cheer him up," Celine, a stewardess, told me. "I make plans for us to go out, or I invite friends over. I tell him he doesn't have to worry because I have a good job and we're not dependent on his income. But he's just miserable no matter what I do."

After trying emotional mirroring, Celine was surprised to find out that being out of work was just the tip of the iceberg. George was depressed because he was out of work, of course, but he confessed that he really didn't like his work at all. He was also upset with himself because he didn't really want another job—there didn't seem to be anything else he could do.

Celine really stopped to listen. She found out that George didn't want to work for anybody, he wanted to be his own boss. He was fed up with directors and producers telling him what to do. "I like my job so much," Celine said, "I just assumed he liked his."

Now, they've just bought a small printing business and George is happily running it. He doesn't make as much money, but he's a lot easier to live with. "I actually heard him singing in the shower last week," she told me. "Now I don't feel guilty for being happy anymore."

The good thing about mirroring a man's emotions is that you will often find out a lot more if he feels you're sympathetic. George told Celine he never said anything about not liking his job because he thought she wouldn't understand. In the past, whenever he'd been upset, she'd just said, "Oh don't worry, honey, everything's going to be fine. Cheer up." Just exactly what he didn't want to hear.

When a man is upset or depressed, he wants to feel justified. Let him know you agree with him, that you sympathize with him, and be sure to find out if there's anything else that's bothering him. Always find out what's wrong. That way you can do something about it.

Be careful not to *get* angry when you are mirroring your mate's anger. Be extra sure to agree in some way with his side of whatever conflict has him angry. Mirroring anger and disagreeing at the same time, or even seeming to, can lead to runaway hostilities.

For example, your husband is angry because you spent more than he thinks you should on the kids' back-to-school wardrobe. He says, "This is an outrageous bill. We've got to stop spending so much." You say (in the same angry tone), "You're right. Kids are too expensive these days. I can understand why you're upset." You have mirrored his emotions without escalating the battle.

Mirroring Volume

Mirroring volume is very simple. It means when he talks softly, you talk softly. When he yells, you yell. Many women have the type of quiet man that can be infuriating. He's the type who hates to fight and hates scenes. He'd do anything, even something he loathes, to avoid an ugly scene.

Randy was like that. He was driving his wife, Stacey, crazy. "I can't stand the way he never gets excited about anything," she told me. "It's as if he just doesn't care." When I asked Stacey what she would do to try to get Randy to open up, she told me, "I've yelled and screamed, I've thrown tantrums. I've even thrown things—and once I actually swung at him. And would you believe, no reaction. Not a thing. He just walks away.

"I ask him about things, simple things. 'What do you think of this carpet sample?' or 'Would you like to barbecue tonight?' Mostly he doesn't answer. He just grunts. Or he says something like, 'Whatever you want's okay with me.' I could absolutely kill him."

I noticed that Stacey's ordinary tone of voice was about two times as loud as anyone else's. When I talked to Randy, he was surprisingly quiet.

Instead of murdering Randy, Stacey gave mirroring volume (and enthusiasm) a try. Even though Randy had fallen in love with Stacey's outgoing personality and loved the way she was able to speak right up to anybody about anything, he himself was shy and softspoken. So the next time she was about to blow up at Randy, Stacey tried matching his nonchalant I-don't-care tone of voice.

"It was amazing," she reported. "The quieter I got, the more he listened."

Mirroring Attitudes

Although I said before that mirroring is not a game of Monkey See, Monkey Do, that applies only to direct physical mirroring. On a different level, we all have a natural tendency to pick up on the appearance, attitudes, and activities of those around us. You can use that tendency to influence your man and improve your relationship.

If you want your husband or lover to be more romantic, make sure you hang around romantic people. Find some newlyweds and spend some time together. You may be surprised to see them act exactly the way you used to. The romance hasn't disappeared forever. You can bring it back.

Mirroring is so powerful that we often mirror people we respect or look up to without even being aware of it. It is a common bond of human experience. Children mirror their parents. Even animals in the wild learn by "modeling" or mirroring. If you want your husband to be sexier, guess what? Take him somewhere to see sexy men.

Does he like James Bond movies? James Bond is always sexy. Find a star he likes and you think is sexy, then go see him together. You'll be amazed at how your husband will adopt the romantic and sexy postures just from unconscious mirroring.

You can help, of course, by telling him how much you like it when he does something romantic or sexy. Your positive feedback will make him want to do it more.

In a very subtle way, the man in your life will be unconsciously influenced when you mirror him. When you start paying closer attention to him and using better ways of communicating, some of this will rub off on him. He'll start to be more attentive to you.

Mirroring to Get What You Want

Mirroring your mate's belief system is the easiest way to get him into a state of agreement. *Always* get him into a state of agreement before you ask for something. That way he's more likely to say yes to whatever you want.

There are probably lots of things the two of you do agree on. There are political beliefs you share, child-rearing methods you both insist on, foods you both love to eat, philosophies you believe in, people you like and don't like, favorite music, favorite television shows, even the way you make love—and when and where.

Sharing so many values makes your life easy and comfortable with your partner. But once in a while, you want to change his mind about something or express your disagreement over an issue.

If you start with the area you agree on and then go to the area of disagreement, you will eliminate a lot of friction and arguments and you'll also get your way more. When you agree with him first, he'll be more likely to agree with you. It's the team spirit that men all tend to follow. "You say I'm right and I'll say you're right."

Getting into agreement is a technique that's used by doctors and lawyers, salespeople and managers. Once you have found the points on which you agree, you can always come back to your agreeable state if you get into an argument—by bringing up the things you agree on.

Perhaps someone you've dealt with has gotten you into a state of agreement before influencing you in some way. Remember the last time you went shopping and bought more than you'd planned on. The astute saleswoman may have said, "Let's see, you're a size 10," and you said, "Yes." Then she said,

"And you're looking for something special," and you said, "Yes, a special party dress." She said, "I have some really special party dresses over here," echoing your words. The dresses may or may not be the kind of special party dress you're looking for, but you're inclined to agree that they are since she's gotten you to say yes to all the other things first.

She has cleverly mirrored your own words. You are, in fact, in a state of agreement with her. And so, without even being aware of it, you trust her when she tells you something looks good on you and you buy it from her.

Getting into a state of agreement with your mate by mirroring his belief systems is easy because, unlike the saleswoman, you don't have to guess at what his belief systems are.

Let's say your husband is a total slug. He hates to exercise and you are a regular fitness queen. It's Sunday morning and you're into your routine—leg kicks, situps, stretches. You desperately want him at least to take a walk around the block with you, instead of just sitting around all day doing nothing but eating and building cholesterol so he can die and leave you with the kids, the mortgage and a middle-aged spread that nobody'll want.

Try not to say, "If you don't walk with me this morning your arteries will finally close off and you'll die by nightfall." Try first mirroring his belief system. Talk slowly, breathe deeply. Say, "Exercise is so boring. (Yawn) I'd rather do almost anything but exercise, wouldn't you?" Of course he would. "I know just how you feel," you tell him. "I feel that way myself a lot."

"You do?" he perks up. "That's funny, I thought you really loved to exercise." You've gotten him into a state of agreement first. Then you can say, "But it would feel so good to have a romantic arm-in-arm walk after dinner. That would make some special time for us to be alone together. We could walk slowly, and afterwards, I'll serve nightcaps in bed."

Sure, you're bribing him. Sure you don't want to walk slowly. But he does. By starting out with your point of agreement you at least have a chance of getting him out walking, if only slowly. Then you may be able to get him to walk a little faster. But you have to get him out of the house, first.

So start by breaking down whatever you want your mate to do into small steps. Sure you'd like him to clean out the garage, but maybe you could start by getting him out there to look at one box of junk or help you move one thing. Then you have a chance to get the rest done. Find an area of agreement—like saving his old fishing equipment from getting warped, then move on to cleaning the whole garage, one small step at a time. Be sure you start the first step by making it in his interest to do what you want done, especially in his Love Language.

As soon as you're both in agreement, he'll begin to feel trusting and confident. Then he'll be more likely to agree with the next thing you say. That's the time to bring up new ideas, to suggest something different, or to broach a problem.

You can mirror anything about your mate—the words he uses, the Love Language he speaks, his eye movements, the rhythm of his breathing, or the beliefs he holds sacred—just pick your area of agreement and let him know about it. When you're irritated with him, when he's done something less than lovable, when you want to lay down an ultimatum or insist on a change, first get him into a state of agreement. You'll be more likely to get what *you* want if you start by reminding him of the things you *both* want.

Anchoring

DID you ever wish for a magic wand that you could wave over your mate's head whenever he was less than his usual adorable self? A fairy godmother's wand that would change him from a snarly, grouchy, grump back into your own sweet love? If so, you may be surprised to find out that a magic wand really exists. It's called "anchoring."

After you've learned to use the skills in this chapter, you will have complete control over your mate's moods. When he doesn't feel sexy, you'll have the power to reignite his flame. When he doesn't feel like going out, you can energize him. When he's uptight, you can get him to relax. When he's unromantic, you can get him thinking about candlelight and moonbeams. Anchoring is the secret key.

You have already established lots of wonderful memories and special loving feelings with the man in your life. Each time you have great sex, every time you go on a romantic trip, you are building your romantic memory bank. You can use anchoring to solidify your love by making sure he remembers every wonderful moment he's had with you. With anchoring, you can make those loving feelings and memories available whenever you want them. You can trigger them whenever you need to.

Anchoring Good Times

Just as a certain way of clasping someone's hand in yours can indicate brotherhood, or a social peck on the cheek can betray a superficial friendship, or a bear hug shows real affection, you can establish a certain touch that will always remind your man of how happy he is with you. Then, you can restimulate his good feelings anytime.

Anchoring is one of the most potent tools for keeping a man in love. It's appeal is subtle, unconscious and irresistible. Here's how it works.

Whenever you and the man you love are having an especially wonderful time together, preserve the feeling of that moment with a special touch. Say special words in a special way. Perhaps just his name said in a particularly loving tone of voice, or maybe a pet name or something silly, or "You turn me on," or "Hi, handsome." Each time he seems really happy, use the same touch and the same words in the same way to establish your good times anchor.

After you have done this several times, your good times anchor will be firmly in place. Each time you use it, you just reinforce it.

For example, the two of you are at the beach. The breeze is cool, the sand is warm and the sun is shining. You are rubbing suntan oil on his back and he is obviously enjoying the perfect moment. You brush the hair off the side of his face and say, "Oh, John, you have the cutest nape." Or, "Hey, handsome, got a date tonight?" Or, "Wanna wrestle?"

It really doesn't matter what the words are, just that you always touch the same place and always say the same words in the same tone of voice. It doesn't matter what spot you pick either, except that it's better to pick a spot you can always reach, even if he's dressed and in a public place. His hand, the back of his neck, or his face or arm are good.

Don't use the upper arm, because people often associate a touch there as something comforting in a time of bereavement.

Don't pick something for your anchor you would be embarrassed doing in front of someone. You never know when you want to invoke the good times anchor. You might need it the next time your least-favorite relatives show up. You might need it when the kids are around.

You can use your good times anchor any time. Let's say your man has a miserable time at work, or that his car breaks down on the freeway, or that he has a terrible fight with one of the kids. He's miserable and it's not your fault, but you're there and you certainly get the vibes. All you have to do is touch the magic spot, say the magic words, and presto, magico, he's smiling! He's your own sweet love again.

It's important to get in sync with his mood first. Mirror him. Say something in his Love Language to let him know you really understand him, and then turn his mood around with your anchor. Let's say your visual man has just walked into the house really upset. You get in sync with his upset mood and say, "I can see by the look on your face that you're upset." Then you touch the magic anchor spot you've preset and say the magic words. Tell him, "It's going to be a beautiful starry night." He'll believe you.

Or if he's a feelings man, you might say, "I can sense that you're upset," and then invoke the anchor. Or, if he's an auditory man, "I can hear by the sound of your voice that you're upset," and touch the magic spot. With anchoring, you can control the mood and tone of your relationship and you can take the edge off problems as they occur.

Toni's husband, Keith, was always a little sad and she was always trying to cheer him up. "The only time he acts happy at all," she told me, "is when he plays with the dog." Instead of feeling jealous of the dog, Toni anchored the happy feelings Keith had playing with the dog. Each time he played with the dog, she found an excuse to "play doctor" with him afterwards.

"Oh look," she'd say. "You have a scratch here. Let me kiss it better." Soon, all she had to do was touch his hand where he was supposed to have a scratch, or some imaginary dirt she was rubbing off, and his mood would get happy again. Instead of resenting his happy times with the dog, Toni learned to transfer the same feelings to herself by setting up a good times anchor.

Anchoring a Memory

Andrea came to me one day to talk about her husband, Brett, who was constantly difficult and critical. "I know it has to do with some problems he's having at work," she told me, "but he's absolutely terrible. He hasn't laughed or joked with me in months. He has no sense of humor anymore about anything."

By the time Andrea came to see me she didn't have much of a sense of humor either. Brett's black mood had wafted over her. She too was critical and unhappy. The first thing I did was to ask Andrea to tell me about a time when things were different between her and Brett, a time when they were happy together.

"It was just last summer." She smiled for the first time. "We couldn't go too far away because Brett had to be in touch with the office, so we rented a house at the beach for a week. It was right on the sand. We would sit and watch the ocean from our living room. Brett was so relaxed. It seemed like all we did was laugh and run on the beach."

As Andrea talked about their happy times together, I could see her body posture change. Her shoulders straightened, her frown smoothed over, and there was a smile on her lips. I reached over and touched her hand to anchor the happy feelings she was remembering.

"Now," I told her, "when you go home, you will be able to remember those happy times when Brett seems to be getting you down. All you have to do is get Brett to remember your week at the beach and you can change his mood as well."

When Brett showed up with his usual dour face and critical disposition, Andrea used anchoring. First she got in tune with him: "I can see why you'd be upset," she told him. Then, casually, she said, "Remember that house at the beach we had last summer? I found some pictures of it."

As she talked about the house, she noticed Brett's face relax. Soon, she saw the tension leave his body. He was beginning to smile at the memory of their summer house. She put her hand on his thigh. Gently she stroked his leg as they looked at the beach pictures together.

Sure he got anxious and depressed and critical again the next day, but she didn't even have to bring out the pictures. All she had to do was stroke his leg and he began to relax and became his old self again.

Sex Anchors

Stephanie, a 42-year-old ad space saleswoman, was married to Greg, a 50-year-old investment banker. When she came to me, her complaint was typical: "Greg works all the time and we don't have enough quality time together." After a few minutes, she admitted that their sex life was great, when they had it. Most of the time they were both so busy, they didn't have time. When they did have time, they were too tired, especially Greg, who had been working day and night to close a big deal.

"I've tried sexy nightgowns, vibrators, all sorts of things. But he just doesn't seem to get interested very often," Stephanie told me. "If I push him about it, he tells me I'm a nag and nagging isn't sexy. I think he's taking all the energy he used to put into sex and our relationship and putting it into his work instead."

In order to get Greg's attention back and to refocus his sexuality, Stephanie used anchoring. The next time he got in one of his rare sexually interested moods, she reached up and touched the back of his neck. "You're so sexy," she whispered. When they finished making love, she continued to rub the back of his neck, then his shoulders.

The next few nights she tried rubbing his shoulders, moving to the back of his neck. He thought she was trying to ease his tension from work and he loved it, but she was really invoking the sexy anchor she had set. Greg never did find out why he felt sexy everytime Stephanie rubbed his neck, he just did.

Anchoring in bed is the most powerful, most exciting thing you can do. Why let a wonderful sex experience just fade into a forgotten memory? Why not use it to build happy anchors with the man you love?

Anchoring to Get Him Excited Again

You have a wealth of memories to draw upon to anchor excitement, interest, even love with your man. Don't be shy. Ask him, "What was the sexiest thing you ever did?" Even if it was with another woman. Or, if he never did anything far out, ask, "What was the sexiest thing you ever fantasized about?" It doesn't really matter. The point is that you're trying to get him back into his sexy, excited state.

Ask your man, "What was your first sex experience like?" or "Tell me about your first girl friend?" or "Tell me about the first time you had sex?" Don't let jealousy of some long-gone love keep you from using your man's sexy memories to your advantage. Get him to remember when he felt aroused, excited, interested. Then, just as soon as you get him to tell you about it, you'll notice changes in his demeanor. His face will relax, his eyes will smile at the memory. That's your cue to anchor his sexy feelings—even if they aren't attached to you at the moment. Don't worry about it.

Even if you have the strong, silent type, watch his face. He doesn't have to say a word. You'll know by his expression he's remembering.

Then a magic thing happens: As he's telling you about the experience, or just remembering without telling you, he'll begin to subconsciously associate the sexual experience from his past with you in his present.

Then, once you've done that seal the transfer from his past to his present and anchor his memory by first getting in tune with him. If he's visual, say, "I can see why that was exciting." If he's auditory, you'll say, "I can hear from the tone of your voice how exciting it was" or "that sounds exciting." If he's a feelings man, say, "I can feel how exciting that was. It gives me tingles all over." Or something similar in your own words.

Next, reach over and touch the spot you've chosen as your sexual anchor spot. Touch him in the special way and *voilà*, you have set a sexual anchor. The next time you want to turn him on, all you have to do is touch the same spot and he gets excited. You have anchored his sexuality and made it available anytime you want it.

Soon, the way you touch him on that particular spot and the pleasure he gets will be identified with the excitement and thrill only you can give. You may want to simply say his name as you touch him, or you may have some secret code words you want to establish as a sex cue. You'll be amazed at how quickly his sexuality is under your control. Your special touch, your special tone of voice, your words will be the only ones that turn him on.

If he's visual, you could say, "You're the handsomest man I've ever seen" or "Just looking at you makes me excited" or "When you look at me, I get a thrill."

If he's a feelings man, you might say, "When I touch your skin, I get a thrill" or "I'm always excited when you're here."

If he's auditory, always say his name in a special tone of voice. Be sure to vocalize when you're making love and then touch his special spot. Say, "You sound so sexy."

Anchor your man's happy feelings, his sexy feelings, his relaxed feelings. Every time he has a pleasant experience, anchor it. That way, you have an arsenal of happiness to invoke whenever you want.

Anchoring to Make Him Feel Better

In much the same way I got Andrea to remember a time when she and Brett were happy together and then anchored that memory, you can help your man when he's feeling down. For instance, he comes home anxious and upset over a promotion he's trying to get at work. You say, "I can see [if he's visual], or hear [if he's auditory], or understand [if he's feelings] why you're so upset.

"Remember when you got the last promotion, how good you felt [looked, sounded]?" Try to reconstruct the memory for him. "We were living at . . ." or "It was right after the baby was born" or "We were sitting right here" or "We celebrated by going out for that expensive dinner."

What you are trying to do is get him out of his blue funk and back into the memory of the previous time when everything was fine. Then, as soon as you see by the look on his face that he's not as tense, anchor the good feeling.

This is a method used frequently by therapists who are helping patients remember good times and forget the bad ones. You can use it to keep your husband happy whenever you need to.

Anchoring to Get Rid of Problems

Just as you can anchor a good feeling with a special touch and special words, you can also anchor a bad feeling. In order to anchor a bad feeling you have to first get it out in the open. Many women think that if they ignore an uncomfortable situation, turn away from a problem, pretend an upset husband is fine, everything will work out. They imagine that if they ignore the situation it will get better. Not true. Ignored problems tend to build up and get worse. The man whose angst is sluffed off feels even more upset.

You can make your problems disappear, but not by ignoring them. The way to make your problems disappear is to anchor them. When you anchor bad feelings or problems, you separate them from yourself and your mate. Here's how it worked for Marla and Bill.

Bill, a 42-year-old internist, married Marla, a 35-year-old nurse, just three weeks after they met. Bill and Marla were still living in her apartment five years later. Marla was eager to buy a house, but Bill kept putting her off and putting her off. Year after year went by. "I'm tired of living in this tiny apartment and throwing away our rent each month and having nothing to show for it," she'd rage. "When are we going to buy a house?"

Bill had been married before and had bought a house. His ex-wife got the house in a very painful separation battle and Bill never forgot about his old house. He had invested so much effort and time remodeling it and making it into his dream house and then he had lost it in the divorce. Every time Marla mentioned buying a house, Bill was overwhelmed by all his old painful memories. He said the very thought of buying a house gave him knots in his stomach.

Marla had already set up his happy anchor, and his sexy anchor and even his romantic anchor. Bill, a feelings man, always responded to her soft kisses and gentle touch. The problem was that every time she stopped touching and kissing, Bill was overwhelmed by the bad memories of his past marriage.

In order to get Bill to disassociate her from his bad memories about the ex, Marla anchored his bad feelings. The next time she brought up the house, and Bill, of course, got upset at his memories of his lost house, Marla didn't argue. Instead of her usual "I'm not her, and it's not my fault she took that stupid house"—or worse—Marla agreed with him, mirroring his belief system.

"You're absolutely right," she told him the next time he started to mourn for his old house. "It was a beautiful house and she was a bitch to take it away from you when she knew how much it meant to you." Then she moved over to the corner of their living room, a space they hardly ever used. Pointing to the small table in the corner she said, "I've heard of women like her who take a man's home and everything. These women don't care about a man's feelings," anchoring his thoughts of that other woman and that other house to the corner of the room.

In the past, Marla was always defending herself and getting into long arguments with Bill about how they could hold title to the house to protect his interests and how she wasn't that kind of woman. This time, after she had anchored the ex and the other house in the far corner of the room, Marla moved away from the area and pointed to herself.

"Then there are other women who treat men with love and respect and would never take a man's house away," she said, pointing to herself and putting the same hand with which she had pointed at the corner on her chest. "Some women are different and would never think of taking anything away from a man they love." She started stroking him and kissing him gently. "Some women just want your love, not your house."

Marla anchored Bill's bad feelings about home ownership to a spot in the living room away from her. By moving physically away from that spot and using the same hand to indicate herself nonverbally as the other kind of woman who doesn't take things from men, she disassociated herself from his painful memory.

Whenever Bill brought up his anger at his ex and his loss of his house, Marla skillfully disassociated herself from his old pain by anchoring it away from her own person. Soon, Bill was able to talk to Marla about a new house without thinking about the old one because she had separated herself from it with negative anchoring.

Negative anchoring is especially helpful if your man has bad memories from his past relationships. By separating yourself from "those other women" and the things they did, you will be able to get him to see you as a new individual, by yourself, not as one of a crowd of women all engaged in the same acts. Use a negative anchor to separate your man from his painful past, especially if that past is standing in the way of your future.

Jim's ex had been an actress. She was a big success, but she was never home and always put her career ahead of her family. When he married Elaine, he thought he was marrying a homebody who would never be jet-setting around the world. Then, ten years later, Elaine began to advance in her career. Each step ahead was preceded by long fights, lingering arguments and resentments. Jim couldn't get his ex out of his mind. So, Elaine used negative anchoring on him.

"A lot of women leave their husbands at the drop of a hat and put their careers first," she said, pointing to a chair they never used. Then, using her special tone of voice and touching his good feelings anchor, she said, "But then there are other women who will always put their men first."

Elaine was able to separate herself from Jim's ex, even though, at first, she'd shown some hesitance. "I want to be supportive of other women. I don't want to put them down," she'd told me. To make herself feel better about not supporting all the other women all the time, she would be sure to make a couple of really supportive feminist statements later to balance what she'd said. It made them both feel better.

There's nothing wrong with separating yourself from another woman's bad behavior. We are all haunted by the hurts of the past. Anything you can do to take away some of the pain from the man you love with positive or negative anchoring will be greatly appreciated. It's a way to help your man "see" your good qualities and not mix up his reaction to you with women by whom he's been burned in the past.

Always place yourself strategically near the people your man likes. If he hates a relative, don't you be good friends with that relative. At family gatherings stand next to the people he loves and he'll always associate you with love. If he hates a business associate, and he sees you in physical proximity to that person, some of that hate could rub off on you. When you position yourself close to people he likes, you will get the automatic spillover from anchors he's already set.

13

Man-Handling Secrets

EVERY woman who has been able to keep her man in love with her told me she developed little secrets for "handling" her man. Here are some man-handling secrets that will work on any man. They range from common sense to modern psychology.

Don't Blame

Sure, he's a jerk. He promised to call if he was late and he didn't. Don't say, "You promised to call and you didn't and you made me ruin the dinner waiting for you." You can get the same message across by saying, "The phone didn't ring, and so I waited for you and the dinner got burned." A simple change in semantics, a different way of phrasing something, can make the difference between a pleasant and unpleasant encounter.

It's just as easy to say, "The car ran out of gas," as it is to say, "You let the car run out of gas." Men are very sensitive to being blamed for things. When you start a statement by saying "You . . . ," he will immediately get on the defensive.

Always blame some other, preferably inanimate object, not your mate. Instead of "You made this place a mess," say, "This place is messed up." Say, "The trash needs to be taken out," not, "You didn't take out the trash yet." "The kids need to be picked up," rather than, "You haven't picked up the kids." Avoid at all costs, "you should," "you didn't," "you have to," "you'd better," "you shouldn't."

If you say, "You didn't fix the leaky faucet," he's sure to get defensive about how hard he works and how he just hasn't had time. But, if you say, "That faucet is still leaking," he's likely to reply, "I know. I meant to get to it. I'll fix it as soon as I can." You've made it the faucet's fault, not his, so he feels more like being cooperative.

Exaggeration

So you mushed his fender. It could happen to anyone. Don't say, "Oh, it's nothing, just a little accident." Instead say, "Oh, the most awful thing happened. You'd better sit down, dear. I don't know how to tell you about this. You're going to be so upset. You'll probably never talk to me again." By this time he's really worried. When you say you just mushed the fender, he's relieved.

Reach and Withdraw

When your husband's not paying attention to something, try the "reach and withdraw" method. You say, "I have something very exciting to tell you, but I think I'll wait until later." Or say, "I have a surprise for you. I'll tell you about it later." He'll begin to want whatever you're holding back.

Ask His Advice

I am really surprised at the number of men who say, "Being needed is the most sexy thing for me." So let your man know you need him. Women with successful relationships allow their men to "give advice."

"I ask his advice even when I don't need it or when he doesn't know any more about something than I do," one woman told me about her obviously in-love mate. "I can tell by the look on his face and the tone of his voice that he really likes it when I do."

Listening to What He Doesn't Say

Whenever you hear words like *it, that, everything, nothing, all* or *this,* your ears should perk up. Don't automatically assume you know what he means by his vague references. Often you'll be wrong.

So save yourself a lot of unnecessary grief and aggravation and make sure you know exactly what he means when he says vague things like, "Nothing around here works." Step in and help him get past his "neurotic stimulus generalization," where he thinks *everything* is horrible because he can't make the can opener work. Say, "Exactly what doesn't work, dear?"

My husband has a habit of yelling from the other room, "What's this thing doing here?" Naturally I don't know what thing he's talking about. Instead of trying to figure it out, I just ask. If your man has a habit of saying things that are vaguely alarming but totally nonspecific, don't react to what he said, just ask him what he means.

Figuring out your own interpretation to some of his generalized ranting can be dangerous as well as aggravating. He says, "I'm really angry." Before you decide it's you who's making him angry, ask, "Exactly what are you angry about?" or "Who made you angry?"

He'll feel cared for and by pinpointing his upset or anger, he'll be able to separate that from the rest of his life, including you. One good thing about pinpointing his anger is that you are no longer in danger of becoming the brunt of it. Another important advantage is that once he vents all his anger, he'll probably relax and get on with enjoying life.

Ask who "they" or "them" are. Find out exactly what he's talking about. You'll be doing both of you a big favor.

Hidden Messages

It's true. Men are basically stubborn.

They are certain to do the exact thing you just asked them not to do.

But perhaps your man isn't just being obstinate. Perhaps he *doesn't* want to do the opposite of what you want him to do. Maybe he hears only part of what you say.

You say, "Don't forget to pick up the boys at Little League." Naturally, he forgets.

He forgets because his mind unconsciously blocks out the "don't" part of your message. All he remembers is "Forget to pick up the boys," and that's exactly what he does.

You can be sure if you tell a man "don't" do something, he'll do it. His mind, like everyone's, is more influenced by the hidden positive command in your message. Advertisers have known this for years. They say, "Don't call us first." You hear, "Call us first." It's always better to tell your man, "Remember to call me," instead of, "Don't forget."

You can slyly use this knowledge to your advantage by intentionally using negative sentences with built-in positive messages when you talk to your mate. Remember, any negative tends to be forgotten; people retain only the positive. For example, you say, "You may not remember how good you felt last year when you were working out everyday, but I do." He hears, "Remember how good you felt when you were working out every day." He eliminates the negatives.

If you make sure the hidden, positive message is in his Love Language, you are more likely to get what you want. Say to your visual man, "You may not see yourself living in Manhattan forever, but the picture may change." To your auditory man, "You may not think big-city living sounds good forever, but you could change your tune." To your feelings man, "You may not feel like you'll be happy living in the city forever, but you could feel different about it later."

You can slightly change the tone or the speed of your sentence to emphasize even more exactly what you want him to hear. Talk slower on the parts you want him to remember. Drop your voice and speed up on the parts you want him to forget.

You can use hidden messages in the question form as well. For example, "Why don't you want to go to the Bahamas?" Say "Why don't" quickly, then slow down and emphasize "you want to go to the Bahamas."

Handling Time Competition and Jealousy

In a committed relationship there's not supposed to be any jealousy. Since he's already married or committed to you, you're supposed to be totally magnanimous about whatever he does. How could you be jealous of a cute new assistant in the office? So what if he takes her to lunch or for a drink after work. You're his wife. He comes home to you. Right? Wrong!

Of course you're jealous. Of course you're upset. You want to be with him, you want his time. Time spent with other people can make you jealous even if it's time spent with your very own children, or his boss, or his work.

The competition for his time can be fierce, and he may put your demands last, because you're supposed to know he's already committed the rest of his life to you. The competition can be his job, Monday night football, his racquetball game on Sunday morning, his fishing trip, some bar he hangs out at—all can make you jealous and rightly so. He's supposed to be there for you. You married him so you could be together and he's always somewhere else, with somebody else.

Sure you can get jealous without there being another woman in the picture. You can get jealous because of all the good times you and he are missing together while he messes around with his buddies or his hobbies.

Many older women I interviewed told me their one regret was that they didn't travel more with their husbands when they were younger and had enough energy and health, because now it's too late for them. They regret the quality time they didn't spend with their men when they were younger. You have a right to fight for that time when you can still enjoy it.

If he seems to be taking it for granted that you'll be there waiting whenever he sees fit to spend time with you, let him know there's competition for your time too. Make other commitments. Volunteer, join a club and become an officer so you have to go. Get the kids involved with something where you have to take them. Let him know you're valuable.

Jealousy is a natural part of love. We all want to possess what we love, to hold onto it, to keep it safe. We want to control the source of our pleasure.

Remember, a man is flattered if you're a little jealous, but he feels smothered if you overdo it. Let him know you care, but not that you're suspicious of his every move. Discuss "time" jealousy with him and ask for exactly what you want. You may be surprised and get it.

You may not want to stop him from going on his fishing trips. You probably just resent that he doesn't take you on a vacation as often as he goes fishing. Tell him you'll send him off happily if he'll spend as many days at the beach with you as he does at the lake with the guys. Getting what you want makes it easier to let him have what he wants.

Never try to tell him he *can't* do something, like stop after work for a drink, or go hunting, or whatever it is he wants to do. Men quickly become resentful and rebellious when a woman tells them they can't do something. It's better to be positive about the situation and tell him what he can do to make you happy. Don't try to stop him from doing what he wants. Instead, negotiate. Get him to do what you want.

All of the man-handling secrets described above will work on any man. Women who have kept their men in love have other secrets, though. These come from getting to know your man better than he knows himself. If you know what to watch for, that's not hard to do.

Over the years, your man has developed deeply ingrained patterns for almost any decision he has to make or any action he will take. For example, he will have a particular way he'll get dressed, what he'll put on first, when he'll shave, even how he dries himself. He'll also have more important patterns that affect his entire life, and yours too. For the most part, he is not really consciously aware of these patterns. If you learn your man's patterns, you'll know exactly when and how to push his buttons.

Gourmet or Glutton

The gourmet only wants one very special thing. He prefers one perfect rose to a whole bouquet of flowers. He'd rather see one outrageously expensive Broadway play than several inexpensive off-Broadway plays. He'd prefer eating out once in a great while at a very expensive restaurant than going out a lot to moderately-priced places.

On the other hand, the glutton type wants lots and lots. He prefers huge eat-all-you-want buffets to small but exquisite servings of nouvelle cuisine. He'd rather have six old cars than one new one. He'd prefer a long vacation with lots thrown in to a short very expensive one.

Conformist vs. Nonconformist

Is your husband the type who will do something just because everybody else is? Will he succumb to group pressure? If so, you may be able to get him on a cruise by simply telling him how many other people he knows have gone and how much they've liked it. But if he's a rugged individualist type who prides himself on *not* being like everyone else, you can talk yourself out of a cruise in one sentence by applying group pressure. The nonconformist has to think it's his idea, or something you and he have come up with together. Get him to brainstorm with you about all different types of vacations, then use the Irresistible Persuasion techniques in Chapter 14 to sell him on the cruise.

Instant vs. Delayed Gratification

Some men have to ponder decisions, others can't stand to leave things undecided. If your man makes decisions on the spur of the moment, he probably requires other forms of instant gratification as well. He's the type of man who suddenly decides he wants ice cream at ten o'clock at night and gets dressed and rushes out to get it. He's the man who wants to take his purchases home with him right away. No long-time layaways or back orders will make him happy.

Or you may have a man who actually prefers to wait. A man who ponders things over and over in his mind and has lots of patience to wait for something to be exactly right.

If your man needs instant gratification, if he's the kind of guy who wants what he wants and has to have it right away, then there's no use trying to get him to wait. Be prepared. When you bring up something with him, he'll want to do it right away. Don't talk about planning a vacation for next year, or even next month. He is only really interested if he's going to go right away.

On the other hand, he's the kind of guy who could decide to buy you a mink and rush off to get it. You could have your mink tomorrow.

If your man is the kind of man who likes to ponder things and go over all the pros and cons before he decides, then use a different strategy. If he's slow to action and able to postpone instant gratification (a more mature attitude in the long run), then you are going to be frustrated if you try to get him to do something right away, or on the spur of the moment.

Let's say you want a new dishwasher. The instant guy will probably be willing to put it on a credit card and buy it right away. He'll want to get the problem solved. But if you have a man who likes to think it over, to find out the pros and cons and research everything about dishwashers, or maybe even have the old one fixed instead of deciding to replace it, you will be frustrated trying to get a new one right away.

By remembering your man's basic nature as far as instant gratification needs are concerned, you can save yourself a lot of aggravation: Don't waste your time and energy trying to convince an instant type to wait. Don't bother trying to get your "ponder it" type to do something right away. Just plant the idea and give him time to think it over.

Joy vs. Fear

Some men are motivated by the promise of some future joy that they will get. Others are more motivated by fear of consequences. If you think about it, you probably have an idea of which most motivates your man. This is another of his decision-making patterns, and it's not likely to change. So you can learn his pattern and use it to influence him.

For example, you want to move to another neighborhood or a bigger house or from an apartment to a house. He's reluctant. Remember to get in tune with him first. Say, "I can see why you don't want to move," to the visual man. To the auditory man, say, "I can hear by the tone of your voice that you don't want to move." To the feelings man, "I can sense that you don't want to move." Then follow that with, "On the other hand . . ."

To your man who is motivated by fear of consequences, you add, "If we don't move, our kids are going to get in with bad influences or involved with delinquents or worse." To your man who is motivated by joy, you say, "If we move, we're going to be so happy," if he's a feelings man. Or say, "If we move, you'll be able to have a better view," if he's a visual man or "If we move, you'll be able to play your music as loud as you want," to the auditory man.

Escapers vs. Dreamers

If you want to motivate your man to do what you want him to do—for his own good, of course, then it's important to understand exactly how he gets moved to action. One man's long-range plan might include escaping from the city. Another man's plan might include moving to a dream farm. The destination for both men might be identical, but they are thinking about it in opposite ways. One is escaping from the city. The other is seeking his dream.

Is your man an escaper or a dreamer? One is no "better" than the other, but their motivations are totally different. If your man is an escaper, you can easily get him to do what you want by pointing out all the current terrible things he'll get away from.

For instance, you want to spend some money fixing the outside of the house. You figure on spending several thousand dollars on landscaping. If your man is an escaper, you say (if he's visual), "Wouldn't you love to get rid of those ugly weeds and not have to look at those dead branches that could fall on your car and scratch it?" If your escaper is auditory, you say, "Wouldn't you like to get rid of those noisy squirrels that make the dogs bark all night long?" If your escaper is a feelings man, you say, "You won't be in danger of falling over dead branches and nobody would get hurt if we cut down the trees out front."

Now let's say your man is a dreamer, a visual dreamer. You say, "Can't you see how beautiful our yard will be with new green grass and beautiful flowers?" Or let's say you have an auditory dreamer. You say, "We could have an aviary in the yard and you could listen to the exotic birds singing all day." Or if he's a feelings dreamer, you say, "You would feel so good sitting out in the yard getting some sun."

You can easily find out whether your man is a dreamer or an escaper by asking some simple questions like, "Why do you want to move to the country some day?" The escaper will tell you he wants to get away from the smog and crime of the city. The dreamer will tell you he wants to sit on his front porch and look at the view.

What He Really Wants

Over the years, you have learned a lot about what's important to your husband. So let's say you want to go on a cruise this year. You've never been on a cruise before and you want to convince him to go with you.

Think about him first. What are going to be his prime objections? My visual husband, I knew, would say he would get fat on a cruise because there would be nothing to do but eat and no exercise. So when I wanted to convince him to go on a cruise, I was sure to overcome his objections first. I got in tune with him by saying, "I can see why you don't want to go on a cruise, but this ship looks different. You can jog all around the deck. And they have a 'Golden Door at Sea' program with a fully equipped gym." I could see that I had his interest. Then I really got him. "Besides, you'll be able to eat as much as you like whenever you like, and then work it off afterwards." I knew he secretly loved the idea of all that food; he just needed to know he could work it off so he wouldn't look fat and feel guilty.

Perhaps your husband would be motivated by endless buffets, or socializing with lots of interesting people, or all the free entertainment or just being allowed to do nothing. If you already know that, don't try to convince him to go on a cruise because of all the great tourist spots you'll see or all the great shopping you can do for Christmas. The truth is he doesn't care and won't be moved at all.

How sad to realize our husbands aren't always motivated by the same things we are. How important to find out exactly what does motivate them, so we can get them to do what we want, avoid conflict and keep us and them happy.

14

Advanced
Man-Handling
Secrets

YOU now know a lot about the man in your life—his Love Language, his habits and patterns, a lot about what makes him tick. You've got a handle on him.

But you can do more. You can get a real lock on him. You are about to uncover his entire decision-making process—what he thinks about, in what order, to reach a decision.

Your Man's Decision Process

Men have different patterns of reaching decisions about different things. If your man is visual, his pattern will probably start with a visual thought. To complete his thought pattern and reach a decision, he will then "touch base" with his hearing and feelings, in some order. You will want to find out what that order is. That's his pattern. Once you learn it, you'll really have a handle on your man.

For instance, let's say you want to find out how he's attracted to something. You ask, "Do you remember the first time you ever saw me?"

He says, "Yes," and you see his eyes dart up or sort of stare off into space in an unfocused way. You have momentarily taken him back to the first time he saw you. He's reliving the visual experience.

Then you say, "Was there any specific thing that first attracted you to me?"

And he looks up and then says, "Oh yeah, your gorgeous red hair."

And you say, "And then what happened next? What was your next thought? Can you remember?"

He looks off to the side and then down.

He says, "Well, I said to myself, I'd like to get to know her better."

"And then what happened?" you prompt.

He says, "I've told you before—I felt tingly all over. I just knew I had to go over and talk to you."

So now you know exactly how your man is attracted to something (and it better not be another redhead). First he has to see something that catches his eye, like your hair. Then he has to have a conversation about it with himself, and then he gets a certain feeling that lets him know he should take action.

Now, all you have to do is re-create that process for him and you can get him attracted to anything—a new house you like, for example. You point out to him, "Look at that big yard. I bet it would be big enough for a pool. What do you think? How do you feel about it?"

You see his eyes look up and then to one side. He has probably made a picture of it in his mind, and then has had a conversation about it with himself. As his eyes look down, you know he's completed his thought process. He says, "You know, that would work. It would be terrific. You want to talk to the broker?"

You may or may not decide to buy the house. But by knowing how his decision-making process works, you've convinced him that the house is indeed attractive. Or to be more exact, you have allowed him to convince himself by invoking his Love Language and other senses in the exact order that makes him attracted.

Everyone's order is different. You can find out your man's particular pattern for any situation. For instance, you want to find out what makes your man feel sexy. You ask your auditory man, "What was your first really terrific sex experience like? Tell me about it." You see his eyes look toward his ears, and he says, "Oh yeah, can I remember!" You can tell by the look in his eyes that he really does remember.

You ask him, "What was the very first thing that turned you on? Can you remember that?" You see him look toward his ears. He tells you, "She said, 'I bet you've had a lot of girl friends,' and just the way her voice sounded excited me."

You ask, "And then what happened?"

And he says, "Well, I really looked at her for the first time and noticed she was very sexy looking."

"And then what happened?" you ask.

He says, "Well, this Beatles song, 'I Wanna Hold Your Hand,' was playing on the radio and I thought to myself, 'I wanna hold your hand,' about this girl, Suzy. So, I took her hand and it felt so good, I got so excited, I could hardly control myself."

You, being a mature and sophisticated woman, won't be jealous about hearing of Suzy, his first love in high school. Instead, you'll use the new knowledge you have of your man's Love Language order for being turned on. You know he has to hear something to get started. You even know that something like 'Hey sexy, I'll bet you've had a lot of girl friends,' will be magic words. And you know that the next thing he'll do is give you a closer look, and then touch you.

If you want to get him even more excited, you'll play the old Beatles song for him. We are all somehow still turned on by the thing that first stimulated us.

You probably remember something from your first sex experiences, too, perhaps the music that was playing or the food you ate, or something you saw, or something he said, or the way you felt afterwards or a special way he looked at you or a special physical characteristic. You may remember it consciously and seek out part of what first turned you on, or you may remember it unconsciously.

You, too, have a particular Love Language order that was formed long ago. The man who gives you some re-creation of the stimulus that you had then is most likely the man you bought this book to find out more about.

If you think back to the first time you were sexually attracted to a man and remember what first attracted you and what happened next and after that, you will pinpoint your own Love Language order for being sexually attracted to a man. If you want to know what makes you fall in love, you will have to remember exactly what happened the first time you fell in love. (And if you want to know what makes you good in a job interview, you only have to remember the last time you were good.)

Just as your patterns are firmly planted, everything about your man is there in his subconscious, firmly implanted, waiting for the next person who accidentally stimulates his Love Language in the exact order that sets him off. Once you have pinpointed his Love Language order, you will have a key to getting him to do whatever you want—and liking it.

Let's say you have your heart set on a particular new car, and you want to make sure he agrees with your choice. After all, both of you agreeing is the essence of a good relationship. So you say to your feelings man, "Do you remember the first car you fell in love with?"

He looks down and says, "I'll never forget that car. I loved that car." You can tell he's wrapped in the memory by the smile on his face.

You say, "Do you remember what happened to make you fall in love with that car?"

He says, "Sure, I smelled the leather and it made me crazy with desire. And then when I rode in it, I felt like I was floating on a cushy cloud."

"And then what happened?" you ask. "Well, we came back to the used car lot and my father looked at me and said, 'It's some super car. You deserve it.' And when I heard those words, I swelled with pride, and nothing could have stopped me from buying that car. I drove her for years. She had a heart like a lion. Nothing stopped her."

So when you take your mate to see the car of your dreams, you say, "Wait until you smell the leather and feel the cushy ride." And then when he's in the car, you look at him and say, "It's some super car. You deserve it." Guaranteed, he's going to love the car you love.

Persuasion by Agreement

Couples stay together because of the ways in which they are alike, not the ways in which they are different. Similar backgrounds, similar values, similar likes and dislikes keep a couple close. In order to stay close, always emphasize the areas of agreement, especially right before you get into an area of disagreement.

Let's say you want to get your man to go shopping for some new clothes, something he's not eager to do. Don't start by telling him all his old clothes are tacky and out of date— even if they are. Don't demand that he throw away the suit with the gangster lapels or the jeans with the bell-bottom legs. Never start out by making him feel you're criticizing him.

Start out by getting into an area of agreement and appreciation. It's a failproof technique. You first say three nice statements that he's likely to agree with. The fourth is not necessarily something he agrees with, but he agrees anyway, so as not to break the nice vibes, just because you've gotten him into an agreeable state.

Lots of people use agreement to get close and develop trust. Your doctor says, "Let's see, you're twenty-nine." You nod. "And you missed your last period." You say, "That's right." She says, "And you think you may be pregnant." You say, "Right." And she says, "Well, that's no problem at all. Just hop up on the table and we'll take care of everything."

Neither of the last statements are necessarily true, but since you've agreed with the first three statements, you're much more likely to agree with the last two. You also will trust a doctor who is in agreement with you more than one who isn't.

You may have run into the agreement technique on a job interview. The interviewer says, "Hmm, you graduated from Yale." And you say, "Yes." And he says, "And you were fifth in your class." And you say "Yes, I was," nodding in agreement. He says, "And you want to specialize in corporate law." And you say, "Yes, that's right." Then he says, "Well, you're lucky if they take you here. You've come to the best corporate law firm in the East." The last part is not necessarily true, but you tend to agree because you've already agreed with the beginning of the conversation.

Another force is active when you get your man into a state of agreement. He hates to change his mind; he thinks only women change their minds. Once a man is agreeing with something, once he's committed his viewpoint and set the tone for the conversation—one of agreement—he doesn't want to change. Nobody wants to disagree with someone who is obviously so much like them. Also, nobody wants to be uncomfortable. It's easier to keep agreeing.

Irresistible Persuasion

You are now ready to get your man to agree with you, and like it. All of the techniques you've learned can be combined into a powerful persuasion strategy. You know your mate's Love Language and his decision-making process, you have set a "good feelings" anchor, you know how to mirror him and get in tune with him, and you've just learned about how to get him into a state of agreement. You will now simply combine these techniques. The result is really potent.

Be careful not to squander this strategy on getting him to take out the trash, or experiment with it on something you're not sure you really want, like moving to Rio or hiking around the world. But when you need to convince your man of something that's important, that you're sure is best for both of you, you'll find this strategy for persuasion is truly irresistible.

For example, let's say you and your man haven't had a vacation for a long time. You're worried that he's working himself into a heart attack, but he won't admit he needs a break. Here's how to get him to agree to take a vacation.

The Six Steps to Irresistible Persuasion:

1. Get in tune with him by mirroring his breathing, posture and mood.

2. Invoke your preset good feelings anchor.

3. First statement—Say something he'll agree with in his Love Language.

4. Second statement—Also say something he'll agree with in his Love Language.

5. Third statement—Say something he'll agree with in a *different* Love Language.

6. Fourth statement—Say something not necessarily true, but which you want him to agree with, in his Love Language.

First, make sure he's in a reasonably good mood to start with, and that you're going to be undisturbed for a while. Invoke some memory triggers, say, snapshots from a previous vacation he loved. This will take his thoughts away from work and get him in the mood.

Mirror him, to be sure you're totally in tune with him, and keep mirroring him throughout these steps. This is crucially important. If he drops out of tune with you, don't proceed. Go back and start over, or wait and try again another time.

Let's say that his Love Language is visual and he is an

escaper rather than a dreamer in his motivations. You touch his good feelings anchor while you're both looking through some vacation snapshots. You say, "Look at this one. We look like a couple of natives!" He smiles. "Sure do." Next, you say, "You sure haven't looked that relaxed recently." "How could I?" he can't deny it. So you say, "I know you've been under a lot of stress lately [the third agreement, in another Love Language]." Then you say, "Let's get away—I can picture you on a sunny beach in Maui, thousands of miles from any business problems." He is bound to agree.

When you are saying the first three statements, the ones you want him to agree with, modify your voice, and talk slowly. Check his face to see if there's an imperceptible nod, or perhaps even a vocal agreement. Give him time to verify the truthfulness of what you're saying in his own experience. Make sure he's still in tune with you.

Since we all yearn for what's comfortable, your man will have subtle psychological pressure put on him to agree with you, simply because when you slip into another Love Language in step 5, he becomes slightly disoriented and uncomfortable. You induce a slight hypnotic state, similar to the way you would feel if I said to you, "What color do you hear?" or "What color do you feel?" or "What feeling do you see?"

This pressure makes him relieved to get back to where he feels comfortable. When you do that, by returning to his Love Language in step 6, he will agree automatically, happily.

In your relationship, there will always be some little problem or disagreement to work out. Sometimes, even though you know he's got lots of objections to what you want, you're determined to go ahead. That's when it's important that you be persuasive rather than argumentative.

First, find out what his objections are if you don't already know. Then, in steps 3 and 4, find a way to make those statements specifically agree with his point of view. That will get you in tune with him, then you can use the irresistible persuasion strategy to make him see things your way. When you use this strategy, you are reaching deep into your man's psyche to find the part of him that wants what you want.

For example, you have decided you would like to start a little business of your own. He has lots of objections. Instead of arguing, you mirror his objections in his Love Language with at least two statements of agreement, then switch to another Love Language for the third agreement, then back to his Love Language for the fourth statement, with which he will automatically agree.

Let's assume your man is auditory. You mirror him. You get in tune with him. You anchor him. Then you say, "What you say about me not listening to your objections is probably true [first agreement statement in his Love Language]." "And I know it sounds risky [second agreement statement in his Love Language] but I can see lots of ways the money would help out around here [third agreement in another, visual Love Language]. You'll never hear me complain again if you go along with me on this [fourth statement in his Love Language, not necessarily true, but with which he'll naturally tend to agree]."

When you begin a discussion by mirroring your man's objections, the first thing that happens is that he really starts listening to you. After all, you're agreeing with him. You're not arguing. He's relieved. He's not busy thinking of his next argument. You're both on the same side. When he hears that you're really listening to him and appreciating his viewpoint, his subconscious stubborn resistance begins to fade. He feels like being agreeable. That allows the persuasion strategy to work.

Suppose you want your feelings man to go to your class reunion with you. He, of course, wants to stay home. You say, "You may not feel that you're going to have a good time [first agreement in his Love Language], and I can certainly understand why you don't want to hang out with a bunch of strangers [second agreement in his Love Language]. I see what you mean [a third agreement in a visual Love Language]. But once you get there, you'll love it [fourth statement, in his Love Language, with which he'll likely agree]."

Weaving It All Together

As you practice mirroring your mate, using his Love Language, triggers and anchors, you will learn more of his innermost thoughts. The more you know him, the better you will get at using these techniques. You will be able to create a state of agreement instantly, at any time. Your relationship will become ever more harmonious, intimate, and secure.

Your man will find a new excitement in being with you, a feeling of happiness and oneness in your relationship that will truly keep him in love with you forever.

15

Winning Without Fighting

SURE, you're likely to have fights. Who doesn't? Somehow we expect to fight with our kids, our in-laws, our siblings and parents, but magically we're not supposed to fight with a man we love. We think once we find someone we love and who loves us, everything will be sympatico from then on.

All couples fight. All couples disagree. What's dangerous is when every disagreement escalates into a bitter battle. When you both say things that can't be taken back. When harsh, cruel words spoken in anger remain in both your minds long after the fight is over. When an argument over who left the toothpaste uncapped or the garbage in the disposal becomes a bitter dispute over who's right and who's wrong, who's the good person and who's the bad person. Then your relationship is in jeopardy.

Constant battles embitter the fighters. No matter who wins, you both bear the scars. Your superficial anger can grow deep, long-lasting roots of alienation. The seeds of doubt you sow can chip away at the foundation of your relationship. When new hurts surface, they are compounded by the old ones that are still remembered.

Psychologists once thought that the best cure for anger and hostility was to get it out in the open, lay it right where it belongs, tell the person who made you angry exactly what you think of him or her. Fighting among couples was held in such high esteem as a way to strengthen a relationship that books were written on how to fight fair, and foam rubber bats were sold so you could hit your partner until you felt better.

Today, we know that getting anger out in battle does not usually make you feel better. It makes you feel worse. The more violently you express your anger, the angrier you become. "Neurotic stimulus generalization" takes place. You start out angry about one thing and you're soon angry at the whole world.

Fighting with your husband is degrading. It can make you cry and then you look all puffy and horrible for hours afterwards. It can ruin a perfectly nice day. Even if you win, it can be a bitter victory.

Win or lose the argument itself, you really lose, because you got upset. Anger causes stress, stress causes premature aging and a host of other symptoms. There's enough stress in our lives today without getting upset with each other.

We all know at least one *"Who's Afraid of Virginia Woolf"* couple who are always sniping at each other and yet seem to stay together anyway. For them, fighting and then making up afterward may be fun just because making up signals the relief of stress. But most sniping, fighting couples eventually break up. Or they find other ways to get even with each other.

They withhold sex, or they purposely undermine their partner's self-esteem, or they become angry lovers playing sadistic games with each other in and out of the bedroom. Even watching them together makes you vaguely uncomfortable and you end up wondering if that could happen to you. So you determine *never* to fight, which won't work either.

Even though fighting is destructive to you and your family, never become a doormat and give in all the time just to keep the peace. If you smother your anger too much, you run the danger of turning your anger inward, getting depressed and hurting yourself. If you live a life of constant compromise where you always let your mate have his way no matter what, you will begin to devalue yourself and your opinions. You'll resent your man for being able to ride roughshod over you all the time, and you'll hate yourself for letting him. You'll lose respect for yourself and so will others.

Never get into a shouting match with a man. Most of the time he can win with sheer volume. Men are just naturally louder shouters. They can drown you out. Neither should you try to fight a man physically or push him until he's out of control. Don't hit and you won't get hit back. If you see the whites of his eyes, don't be stupid. Back off. Everybody has a breaking point.

You shouldn't have to either give in or fight all the time. There are ways to do battle subtly, quietly, sensitively. By saying the right words, you can maintain closeness in the face of anger.

Reflecting

If you can, get into agreement, even about his anger. Say, "I can see why you're angry," if he's visual. Or if he's auditory, "I can hear how angry you are." Or, if he's a feelings man, "I can sense how upset you are." Don't get angry back. Don't let him think you think his feelings are unjustified or that he has no right to them.

When you reflect your man's feelings, you do several things. You help him because it's so hard for men to talk about how they feel. You defuse his anger, because you're agreeing with him. You keep him from being defensive because you aren't arguing. You let him know you're on his side.

Let's say he's angry because you forgot his birthday. Instead of defending yourself, which only makes you feel tacky, or attacking back, which will escalate the argument, agree. Help him express his real feelings. Say, to the visual man, "I can see that you feel unloved because I forgot your birthday."

To the auditory man, "It sounds like you feel unloved. . . ."
And to the feelings man, "I sense that you feel unloved."

When you do this, you agree with him. He can't very well continue fighting with you if you agree with him.

Venting

Venting is a way of getting your partner to tell you what's really bothering him. He's not really picking a fight because you're out of coffee or because you forgot to tell him his friend called while he was out. You know something else is bothering him. If you let him just walk around collecting examples of alleged injustices you've committed, pretty soon he'll throw the entire list at you. It's important to get things out in the open.

By getting all his grievances out in the open, you do him a service. He no longer has to walk around remembering all the things that bother him. You do yourself a service, too, because living with him gets a lot easier.

Instead of telling him to go out and buy the coffee himself or that people forget to give phone messages sometimes, tell him, "I guess I just forgot. So what else is bothering you?"

You may be surprised. You may hear more than you bargained for. One woman's husband told her, "Our sex life is terrible."

Instead of getting upset, she said, "What exactly about our sex life is terrible?"

"You're always too busy. When I want to make love, you always have something else to do."

She said, "Well, maybe you're right. I have been really busy lately." But she could see that he was still upset. So she said, "What if we made love more often, would that be better?" By asking him what would happen *if* that problem went away, she got him relaxed and over what he saw as an insurmountable conflict.

He shrugged. "I guess so."

Then she said, "Is anything else bothering you?"

Finally, he admitted, "Well, now that you mention it, there is."

So she asked, "What is it?"

And he said, "Well, you used to kiss me when I came in, and now you don't do that anymore."

Next, she asked, "What if I did? Would everything be okay then, or is there anything else on your mind?"

Finally she got his whole list of grievances. Some of them went back five years. Afterwards, they both felt as if a weight was lifted from them. She told me, "We didn't fix everything right away, and some of the things he was upset about were too far in the past, but just talking about everything put our marriage on a much more even keel."

Even when there's nothing obviously wrong, it doesn't hurt to sit down with your husband and talk things out once in a while. Ask him if anything's bothering him.

Many complaints lose their fire after you let them explode. Never let them fester and stay hidden. You can deal with a complaint if it's out in the open, but you can't do anything about it if it's hidden.

Self-Disclosure

Self-disclosure is a way of saying to the man in your life, "Yes, I know how you feel because I've felt that way too." It's a way of building rapport and closeness and of reassuring him that you accept his revelations.

He says, "You drive me crazy waiting. You're always late. You know it upsets me. Can't you be on time just once?"

Don't give him excuses for why you're late. Don't promise to change immediately and forever, which you might not do. Instead, try some self-disclosure. Tell him, "You know, it drives me crazy too when I'm late. I don't know why I do it. It seems like no matter how early I start, I manage to be late."

Then, throw the problem back in his lap. "What do you think I should do?"

"Try just getting it together sooner. Or maybe you need to organize your things better," he says.

Now instead of being absorbed with the problem, he's involved with the solution, a much more productive activity. And, for the moment, you are off the hook.

Say It First

You know when he's about to complain about something. You can sense it. The kids are out of hand. The house is a mess. He's not getting enough sex. The bills are too high.

Jump the gun. You complain about whatever it is before he gets a chance to. All he can do is agree with you when you do this.

For instance, you've lost your keys and have to go out. You say, "Do you mind if I take your keys, dear?" He says, "No," but you can see by the look on his face that he really is not pleased. You know he's about to lecture you about keeping your keys in one place. You can tell by the rigid set of his jaw, the slight drawing together of his brows.

So you look him straight in the face and say, "I know you hate it when I take your keys. But I won't be gone long."

This is a very clever strategy. You have defused his anger by getting right to his feelings. You have beaten him to the punch, so to speak, and you have clearly overcome his objections by telling him you won't be gone long. If he still looks about to lecture, you say, "I'm going to start putting my keys in one place as soon as I come in, from now on."

Now he has nothing left to do but agree with you. Once again you have sidestepped a potential argument.

Since men consider home a sanctuary from the world, they prefer peace and quiet and no stress at home. They don't really want to get upset and angry. By sidestepping his anger and staying in agreement with him, you are really doing your relationship a great service. You are also keeping yourself and your man alive longer.

Winning with Humor

Using humor is one of the best ways to destroy an argument. I have always been a crazed shopper. My closets are always bulging and my husband Marshall hates to see me coming toward the house with armfuls of packages. Whenever I go on a book promotion tour, I head for my favorite department store between talk shows. Shopping relaxes me. It's my entertainment.

Naturally, Marshall hates to shop and can't understand why I love it. He's always complaining, "This house is full of junk. There's no room for anything else."

No use arguing with him. He's right, but he doesn't understand my need for something new every once in a while. And it doesn't help to argue or try to explain. So I've been using humor with him. "I've won the shopper of the year contest," I tell him or "They've given me a storage space attached to the mall and that's where I'm keeping all the rest of the stuff until we build an extra room." Or I say, "I had to buy a present for your mother, for next Christmas" or "Mr. Saks called me and told me they needed me for their year-end budget to come out right" or "I'm helping the recession." When I came home from a tour in England and Ireland, loaded with heavy Irish sweaters and a Burberry raincoat when it hadn't rained or been under 90 degrees in Southern California for months, I told him, "I've been helping save the queen."

Of course, he was still upset with me for buying more stuff, but it's hard to snarl at humor.

Futurizing

Sometimes all a man needs is to be reassured that whatever is bothering him won't go on forever. I use futurizing a lot. When I'm working on a book, I tend to let everything else go. The whole house gets covered with my papers: notes here, chapters there, extra copies everywhere, research piled up, unanswered mail, unread magazines. Eventually, Marshall starts to complain. "There's no place for me to put my briefcase down," he growls accusingly.

"I know how you feel," I sympathize. "There's no place for me to put my briefcase down either. But as soon as the book is done, it'll all get cleaned up." He may still grumble a little, but the promise that the mess won't last seems to keep him happy.

Of course, he uses the same techniques back on me (one of the dangers if your husband starts to catch on). If I'm raging about needing new carpet because our old one looks so terrible, he'll say, "I don't like it either. As soon as you finish your book we can have it replaced." Or, if I'm bothered by workmen in the house, he'll say, "It's a little problem now, but you're going to be so happy with our new quiet furnace next year."

Use futurizing in your man's Love Language. For instance, your man is resisting buying a new refrigerator even though your old one is on its last legs. To get into agreement with him first, you say, "I know the old one is still running," to your visual man, "but can't you see the kitchen with a modern beautiful refrigerator." To your auditory man, "You'll love it when there's no noisy motor running day and night." And to your feelings man, "You'll be so happy with all the good food we'll be able to eat."

The Broken Record Technique

When you use the broken record technique, you don't argue. You get into agreement first by letting him know you understand his point of view. The broken record technique is especially effective when you feel as if your man is trying to bully you into something you don't want to do.

David, a lawyer, was always telling Jill what was wrong with the way she ran her business and what she should do about it. Jill, whose chain of discount clothing stores was doing very well without David's help, resented his trying to butt in and push her around. He also wanted to be totally in charge in almost every area of their lives, especially how they spent their money and made investments. David wanted to expand her clothing business.

At first, Jill argued with him on the basis of women's lib, and her success without his advice, and especially defended her investment acumen. Jill was furious when she told me about it.

"I am not ready to expand. I can hardly handle what I have now and keep it under control. But no matter how I try to explain that to David, he isn't convinced. He wants to build an empire, right away. He wants to franchise my stores. I want to keep the small personal operation I have." I suggested the broken record technique. It worked like magic.

Instead of arguing with David, Jill said in a calm and pleasant way, "I can see why you might feel that way, but I want to keep the business the way it is for right now." Or she'd say, "I can see how it's an interesting idea, and I'll certainly think about it, but I want to keep the business the way it is right now." Or she'd say, "It looks like a good idea, but I want to keep the business the way it is right now."

Eventually David got tired of shouting and ran out of arguments. He couldn't argue back with Jill because she was no longer giving him any ammunition.

Jill also used agreement. She would say, "Yes, you're right, maybe I'm too conservative, but I'm going to keep the business the way it is for right now."

These various techniques for getting your man to stop fighting and start listening have nothing to do with giving in. They are ways to get what you want and to stand your ground without arguing. When you get on the same wavelength as your man, he will be less belligerent, more flexible, and less likely to sulk over not getting his way. He's much easier to persuade when you agree with him first, even if it's agreeing about a negative condition.

Negotiating

If your man is as stubborn about something as a dog with a bone it won't give up, if he's determined to battle until he gets his way on a point, if he absolutely won't compromise, postpone, or forget about it, then negotiate.

If he's dug in his heels, if his jaw is stuck out, and there's no way he's going to back down, if you're going to have to give him his way, at least get something you want out of it. Think of it as a way to keep the give and take working fairly in your relationship.

Now this doesn't mean that you hold out for a diamond every time you have his poker group over. It means you should get a concession of equal value, a reasonable, rational compromise on his part.

You can set up the kind of win-win negotiation that strengthens a relationship. First, you change your negative complaints to positive requests. For example, he says, "You aren't sexually aggressive enough." And you say, "You never take me out or romance me anymore." Complaints that start with the word *You* are usually going to make the other person defensive. It's better to start with the word *I*.

So ask him to tell you what he wants, and he might say, "I would like you to be more sexually aggressive." If you change your complaint to a request, such as, "I would like you to take me out and romance me more," you've both taken a large, positive step toward resolving the issue.

Even complaints that start with "I" and become negative complaints have to be changed to a positive tone before they can be negotiated. For instance, he says, "I wish you wouldn't leave the gas tank empty all the time." You say, changing his complaint for him, "I'll fill the car if you'll wash it" or "I'll fill the car, if you take the kids to the park" or "I'll promise to fill the car, if you'll promise to take the trash out."

If you have a relationship with a man who refuses to negotiate and who won't respond to any of the other techniques for avoiding fights, you will either have to try shock treatment (Chapter 17) or drag him to a therapist or find one for yourself. Giving in all the time is bad for you and eventually will rot your self-esteem. All relationships are a constant series of negotiations and compromises. It's important that you don't do all the compromising. He has to do some too.

So, pick your shots carefully. Most long-married couples have decided that not everything is of equal importance; not everything that you can't compromise over is worth the effort and strain of fighting. Don't make everything a life-or-death issue. You'll both feel a lot better about yourselves.

16

Lovable Slobs

MAYBE your best friend has one, maybe you have one . . . a man who isn't perfect. Probably we all have one. The problem is that there are no perfect men. There are just the ones we have.

If you are stuck with one of these "lovable slob" types, well, it's really not so bad. With a little change in your outlook, you may be able to change his. With the techniques in this book, any woman can positively influence the man in her life to change himself.

But don't plan on changing a dyed-in-the-wool jock into a poet. It's more trouble than it's worth. Besides, for every woman who complains about her mate's normal human weaknesses, there's a woman with the opposite complaint.

For every slob, there's a neatnik who can't stand a hair out of place or a wrinkle.

For every workaholic there's a lazy lout who won't lift a finger.

For every macho thrillseeker, there's a passive wimp.

For every life of the party, there's a stick in the mud.

For every Mama's boy, there's a mother hater.

For every pennypincher, there's an easy mark.

For every scoffer, there's a true believer.

For every Peter Pan, there's an old grump.

187

Here are some of the men wives complain about the most, but who really are lovable in spite of their failings.

The Jock

No matter what, don't come between him and his workout. You know the type: He waits all week so he can run with the dog on the weekend, while you wait all week for a romantic Saturday afternoon picnic. In your whole time together you've never stayed at a romantic bed-and-breakfast inn because they don't have pools big enough for lap swimming.

He's the first one up in the morning, to run five miles before breakfast. You can hardly look at him without worrying about your thighs.

The bathroom is always steamed up when you're putting your makeup on to go out together because he just came from finishing his 200 sit-ups and needs a shower.

The bright side is that he's really clean. And healthy. You may be one of the few old ladies among your friends with a living husband. Look at the alternative. Without his workout he'd be grumpy, nervous, sickly, and downright disagreeable. Besides, the girls always vote him Cutest Buns.

Don't let him intimidate you. Buy Haagen-Dazs, double-stuffed Oreos, Big Macs. Eat them in front of him. Let him know you love your thighs.

The Cuddly One

Some people call it cuddly, you call it fat. His weight is a bigger secret than where Jimmy Hoffa's body is buried. You worry all the time that he's going to die from runaway cholesterol, while he thinks he looks like a sexy Orson Welles. His biggest worry in the world is what he's going to eat next. He has a lifetime membership in Weight Watchers, Overeaters Anonymous and Thirty-one Flavors—and, to your knowledge, he has never missed a meal.

What's really amazing is that you never see him eat anything fattening and yet he can never wear the same pants two months in a row. You never see him do it, but food mysteriously disappears around the house. The candy dish you set out for company is invariably empty by the time company comes, and the dessert always has ingenious, well-disguised slices taken out before it reaches the table.

His idea of exercise is opening and shutting the door to the refrigerator. His favorite activity is grocery shopping or looking for new restaurants.

With this man, though, you'll never starve. If a famine comes, you'll be well fed. He has enough chocolate stashed away so that you'll never be depressed. Besides, he's soft and sweet and oh-so-irresistible to hug.

His idea of love is to feed you. But be careful—if you get fat, he'll be the first one to complain.

The Organizer

His only obstacle to having everything perfect is simply the fact that he personally can't do it all. If he loaded the dishwasher it would be done right. There wouldn't be that water left on the top of the cups. If he wrote all the checks, the checkbooks would always balance. If he did the shopping, you'd never run out of anything. If he taught the kids, they'd be getting all A's. Unfortunately, he's a perfectionist, but never say a word like "workaholic." He truly believes it refers to all those other people.

Whatever you do, don't let him suck you into his drive for perfection. He probably fell in love with you in the first place because you were a lifetime project for him. Without you, he wouldn't be really challenged. Deep down, he knows it. So be mad, be crazy. Mix the teaspoons with the tablespoons. Refuse to fold your underwear. Let him pair up the kids' socks if he thinks it's so easy.

The Midlife Crisis Case

You know he's having it when you have to fight him for space in front of every mirror in the house. You know he's having it when he suddenly decides he needs a whole new wardrobe, gets a blow dry and a manicure, joins a gym, and refuses to let the kids call him "Pop" in public places.

He thinks you should get a new hairstyle. He buys Grecian Formula for his hair, wants hair transplants for his bald spot, gives up his martini for Perrier, and puts a tape deck in the family car. He wants to know if you like his legs and if you think his rear is still cute.

He thinks you should sell the house, buy a boat and sail around the world, or maybe go hiking in Katmandu. He worries all the time about all the chances he turned down to have affairs and hopes he'll keep getting offers.

He wants new friends, new music, new movies, new books, and new sexual experiences. You try to tell him he's already had them all, but he's sure the younger generation has a sex act he hasn't found out about yet. He wants to try marijuana, cocaine, designer drugs, and possibly LSD. He doesn't understand why you are so rigid.

You can always have a midlife crisis of your own. Get a punk haircut, buy heavy metal jewelry, have your ears pierced four times, wear a black leather miniskirt and Madonna top. Tell him you're thinking of starting a second family.

The Sports Nut

He would rather spend a beautiful day watching television than anything else. He knows every team, every player. For him, sports are therapy. When he's cheering the home team or booing the visitors all his troubles disappear. He knows more intimate family secrets about the players than you know about the folks on "Dallas."

In twenty years, he hasn't missed a home game or Monday night football except for your honeymoon, and then he kept trying to turn on the car radio to get the score. If you could, you'd burn his season tickets, tear off his I LOVE FOOTBALL bumper sticker, and get a deprogrammer for him. But you know he'll never stop.

He considers sports part of being a man, some sort of innate heritage, one that's sacred and strictly male. Your part, should you wish to accept the assignment, will be bringing pretzels and cold beer to the den and cheering from the sidelines for his team at Saturday afternoon softball games.

Consider it cheap therapy. If he didn't rant and rave at the tube, who knows what he would do with all that energy—fix the back fence, play with the kids, take the dog to the vet? Then again, he could opt for sex, drugs, and rock 'n' roll.

Figure you're lucky. At least you know where he is.

The Flirt

You feel pretty sure he'd never *do* anything, that it's just harmless flirting. At least that's what he always says. But it bugs you anyway, especially when he starts drooling at someone he always said wasn't his type.

Sure he tells you he likes the natural look. He hates shiny lips, gobs of mascara, black eyeliner, and sleazy clothes. He loves you just the way you are. He loves small breasts, and those extra few pounds just make more to love. And older women turn him on.

And then he practically falls all over some skinny teeny-bopper bimbo with big tits, tons of makeup and a see-through outfit. All your girl friends think he's just great because he always flirts and flatters them. If there was a place in the *Guinness Book of World Records* for hugging and kissing strange women, he would be the winner. He has a way of acting as if he's always turned on and ready for a sexual olympics, but only you know he's perfectly happy with once a week and then off to sleepie-bye.

Of course, if you get mad at him, he just flirts with you too, and he *is* irresistible when he flirts. And when you tell him how unhappy his flirting made you, he gives you those bedroom eyes and that warm, practiced hug that makes all the girls wish their husbands were so affectionate. That's why you always forgive him. But make sure he knows if he goes too far, there will be definite repercussions.

The Super Slob

If there were an Olympic event to see how quickly someone could mess up a kitchen, bathroom, living room, or bedroom, even a closet or hallway, he would win. He can't do anything without making a mess.

He has never picked up a sock, hung up a shirt, towel, or pants, or even noticed when something is dirty. If it weren't for you, he'd go out looking like a Bowery bum with dribbles down his front, mismatched socks, and his belt missing half the loops. Whenever you see him, you automatically scan for miscellaneous smudges, threads, and just awful-looking fuzzy things.

Given a choice between something old, dirty, out of style, and just funny looking, or something clean and together, he'll always choose the strange and scuzzy. He never heard of someone cleaning out a shower. After all, "Doesn't the water do that?" he wants to know.

His favorite things are eating with his fingers, going all weekend without shaving and, of course, dirt biking in the mud.

The good news is you always know what he's been doing because he leaves tracks everywhere. You can also always find him because you can follow the trail.

The Wheeler-Dealer

He always has a new business scheme that's going to make millions. Naturally, you have to type the proposal, answer the phones at home and pretend to be a secretary, run to the Xerox machine and the post office and sharpen his pencils—not to mention entertaining would-be investors and pretending you think hybrid shrimp growing on people's roofs will make a fortune.

He would do just about anything to get out of his regular job, if he has one, and if he doesn't have one, he spends most of his time figuring out how to avoid getting one. Sometimes you'd be glad to give up the alleged joy of venturing for a little security.

His former ventures have left behind a residue of old filing cabinets and office furniture. Your garage has more beat-up desks in it than the state unemployment offices. You have enough old letterheads to supply scrap paper to all the first graders in the United States for the next twenty years.

But he's so lovable and so cute when he's excited about a new deal, and he somehow manages to convince you there's at least a million or two to be made. His enthusiasm is catching and, who knows? Someday, the shrimp might really grow on the roof. So you type one more proposal and dream with him about airplanes and vacation condos, beach houses and the ranch, and someday, a garage you can actually park a car in. The good part is you really could be shopping at Gucci next year.

The Stick in the Mud

His favorite song is "I won't dance, can't make me." For years he has managed to avoid dancing at discos, weddings, bar mitzvahs, anniversaries and other assorted affairs. Whenever there's an invitation to anything that includes dancing, you're supposed to leave him out automatically. The reason is he never learned to dance and, besides, he'd really rather stay home with his model airplanes.

You've tried dancing lessons, getting together informally with other couples, and even joining social groups. But he really isn't crazy for people at all, and since most places where you go out have people, he would rather you went without him.

What he'd really like is to build the fence around the house so high that he'd never have to see anyone other than those few members of his immediate family he thinks are okay and one or two select friends.

The good news is you never have to worry about wearing the same thing twice in a row somewhere, because you go out so seldom people don't remember your name, let alone what you wore. You never have to juggle your social calendar because it's so empty, and you don't have to worry whether you've gained weight since people last saw you. They won't remember that, either.

The Executive

You didn't know when you married him that he was already married—to his job. He doesn't have time for you, the kids, or himself. And it's hard to object. After all, he says, "I have to make a living for all of us." His idea of a vacation is for you to host a convention hospitality suite in Huntsville, Alabama.

When he's home, he says things like, "Haven't you gotten the stereo fixed yet?" or "Can you take the car in while I'm gone?" He's never there when anything starts to leak or breaks.

He has never seen the inside of the emergency ward, while you have been an ambulance driver for so many bleeding children all the emergency-room nurses are old friends. He has never been around for a pet funeral either. By the time he gets home, the emergency is over and he thinks you're making a big fuss over nothing.

He has never seen a school play, gone to a PTA meeting, cheered at Little League, or been to the Brownies. He never misses the kids' birthdays, because his secretary remembers for him, but he forgets how old they are.

He really needs very little. After all, he lives on his expense account. He trusts with absolute faith that he can give you his whole paycheck and that you'll pay the taxes, balance the checkbooks, take care of the mortgage and bills, and do whatever's necessary with the rest. But listen to him yell if something goes wrong. His job is to bring it in, your job is to manage it.

The good thing about him is he doesn't cheat. Not on the company, not on you. If he has any spare time, he tries to get caught up on work, of course.

The Helpless Hunk

He can't find the mustard because it's behind the milk, and he'd never think of moving the milk. He's sweet and always says he's willing to help, but he can't do the wash because he doesn't know how. If you let him try, you know everything white will be either pink or gray, your best woolen sweater will be run through the hot wash cycle, and everything will be two sizes smaller.

He'd be willing to help out in the kitchen, too, but he burns things in a curious way, so whatever he cooks is bonded forever to the pot. And you always worry when he takes the kids out whether he'll bring them all back and how much blood there will be on them.

When he coached Junior League hockey, he broke his leg. When he trimmed the hedge, he stunted it forever. You don't dare let him do any work on the roof, and an electrician is always cheaper than an electrocution.

The nice thing is that you've become very competent, out of self-defense. You can work a pipe wrench, stop a drip, fix a blinking light, drill, saw and even solder. You can do all these things in record time—while he's out of the house.

The Super Star

Everyone loves him because he's seems perfect: a wonderful husband, a great father, the leader of the Elks club, president of his Toastmasters Club, an industry scion, a Cub Scout leader, Little League coach, church leader, fund-raiser and all-around pillar of the community. He helps the elderly widow with her trash cans, changes a fuse for the divorcee down the street, takes in mail and newspapers for the neighbors when they're away on vacation and drives everybody's turn at carpool whenever anyone can't make it.

In front of people, he's "Mr. Perfect." They'd never suspect how snarly he can get in a good argument, because you're the only one who ever sees him moody, grouchy, argumentative or just plain nasty. Let a stranger call, even in the middle of a fierce argument, and he puts on his nicey-nice happy voice, and talks to them in saccharine sweet tones. What really makes you angry is when your own mother takes his side in an argument.

It doesn't pay, though, to get angry with him, because nobody would ever believe he could do anything wrong. At least you know he'll always be nice in public.

The Techie

Congratulations! You are the only one in your neighborhood with two satellite dishes, three video recorders, four computers, a phone system better than Ma Bell's, a clock that tells time in milliseconds, three stereo systems and four televisions, most of which you can't work and don't want to learn.

Instead of worrying about him running away with another woman, you worry about another computer or, God forbid, a kit to make a computer. When that happens, he's bye-bye for months, analyzing it, building it, then familiarizing himself with it until he knows more about the new machine's likes and dislikes than he does about yours.

It's infuriating the way he listens to its every little bleep and whir and never hears anything you say until the third time and you're shouting. You yearn for just a few minutes without any motors humming, while he never seems to notice them at all. Just once, you'd like to be able to talk to him without the background sounds of electronic ecstasy.

Your house looks like the inside of an electronics store. If your living room had any more wires in it, you'd have the copper market cornered. The den looks like a ham radio club is operating there, and you never have any money left over for vacations because he has to have each new gadget as soon as it comes out.

The next time you're alone in bed waiting for him to finish just one more disk copy, tell him you're going to throw the main electric switch if he doesn't come right away. Pulling his plug is the only thing he really worries about.

The Good Ole Boy

He's as lovable and sweet as a St. Bernard puppy and wants to be around you all the time, fleas and all. When he plays softball on the weekends, he insists that you be there to cheer him on and hold his car keys, his beer, his pocket change, and his wallet. Sitting in the sweltering bleachers, choking on dust, you wonder what you're doing there with your master's degree.

The good ole boy is a real authentic macho man who wants the world to know that you are his "woman." He's had his arm hooked around your neck so long your head has a permanent lean. His arm is always there, on the street, sitting in a restaurant or on a barstool, forcing you to stand and sit on a little tilt.

If you ever told him you need more privacy or space, he'd assume you were meeting someone behind his back. But there is a special thrill to having the protection of your big bruiser and knowing he'll always be there. Besides, it's flattering to think that no matter how old, wrinkled, or fat you get, he'll always have his arm around your neck—as long as there's enough Bud in the house.

The Captain

He'd be really happy if only you could run a home like a military barracks. After all, even new recruits learn to pull the sheets until a quarter bounces on the bed. 'And why can't you remember to dust the tops of the doors? His favorite thing is running his finger through dust and holding it up for you to see.

You have to stop him from taking the kids and dog on forced marches. He has a plan of action for every household chore and an assignment for each family member. You have to remind him constantly that a 2-year-old isn't old enough to enlist. Sometimes you want to talk to your own recruiting officer or maybe go AWOL.

You haven't spent a night in a fancy hotel since your honeymoon. His idea of a fun vacation is camping out bivouac style where he gives orders and supervises while you and the kids struggle to put the tent up and have the extra thrill of cleaning fish and cooking on a campfire. Building character is what he calls it. You have other names.

The nice thing about the captain is that he has a strong sense of morals and ethics. He will always do the honorable thing, and that means he'll be faithful, pay his bills on time, and work hard.

The Dreamer

He's really a poet, deep in his soul, too sensitive for this cruel world. He needs you to deal with the harsh realities of life, like making money, paying bills, doing dishes and cleaning house. He stops so often to smell the roses, he doesn't have time to get much else done.

Sometimes he acts so helpless you could scream. He's such an easy mark, anybody can sell him anything. You don't dare depend on him for the simplest acts. Taking the car to the shop or dealing with a door-to-door salesman are over his head. He buys anything from anybody. Last year, you got an award from the Girl Scouts because he bought so many cookies.

No matter what goes wrong, he has a woo-woo explanation. It's in his chart. Or he threw the I Ching and that's what he got. Or he's living out a trauma from a past life.

On the other hand, he's never angry. He's always ready to hug and kiss and love. He gives a great massage, and he really thinks you're perfect just the way God made you.

Lovable Slob Survival Tips

The main reasons we get upset at our own lovable slob are that we find ourselves catering to him, taking care of his needs and putting him first all the time, because after all, we do love him. That's why lovable slob survival tips are about taking care of you. It's amazing how a little time spent pampering yourself will make you feel better about putting up with him. So:

1. Have lunch with a girl friend. Drink a couple of glasses of wine, complain about your husbands, and

then go shopping and buy something wonderful. You'll be surprised how much more lovable your "slob" will seem afterwards.

2. Be generous in spirit. Always keep in mind that he's doing the best he can under his circumstances, and whatever he's doing, it's better than having an affair or skydiving.

3. Get a manicure, pedicure, facial and/or get your hair done.

4. Go out to lunch with a single friend and listen to her awful stories of the dating world.

5. Get rid of some of your domestic duties. Hire a cleaning person. Take all the clothes to the laundry. Eat out.

6. Find an exciting new hobby, volunteer work, a part-time or full-time job.

7. Enter contests and fantasize about winning a Love Boat cruise or a trip around the world. Who knows? You just might.

8. Plan a party for your birthday, anniversary, or favorite holiday. Do it your way. Invite who you want.

9. Do something totally selfish each day, even if it's just a small thing. Ask yourself at the end of each week, what did I do nice for myself this week?

10. Remember, he could be a lot worse, and nobody's got a perfect mate.

17

Shock Treatment

IF the man in your life isn't perfect, that's okay, but if you or your children are suffering because he's a drunk, a cheat, a gambler or physically abusive only shock treatment will get him to change. Shock treatment is called for when all else has failed—you can't get him to stop his abusive behavior and you can't get him to accept help.

At that point, he's learned that your threats are empty. He's decided you won't leave him, and that he can live with your unhappiness. His bad behavior has become habitual. You must make a basic change in this man. The other techniques in this book, which are based on improved understanding and communication skills, will not do that.

Only one thing will change ingrained bad behavior: repercussions. The repercussions of continuing the bad behavior must be worse than the trauma of stopping (or of accepting therapy). As unpleasant as it would be for him to change his ways, you must make it *more* unpleasant for him if he continues them.

Problems involving substance abuse or physical abuse or emotionally disturbed men shouldn't be tackled alone. In addition to shock treatment, help. But for just plain bad behavior, repercussions can provide a quick cure.

Just Out of Line

The principle of repercussions applies even in the case of persistent, everyday rotten behavior, like leaving all the chores for you when you're both working. Or flirting just a little too much at a party. Or coming home late without calling. First, don't pretend that his rotten behavior is okay. Let him know it's not acceptable. Fear of repercussions keeps most men in line. Pretending everything's okay is a signal to your man to go ahead and do whatever he wants.

It's human nature. Generally people will do whatever pleases them if they feel they can get away with it. If your man thinks he can get away with a lot, you can be sure he'll try. It's really not his fault, it's just a natural part of both men and women. We all would like to eat hot fudge sundaes all the time, or pizza, or Dove Bars, or lox and cream cheese, or French food with butter sauces—except that we know there will be repercussions—we'll gain weight or become heart attack candidates.

So if your husband is way out of line and refuses to compromise or change, you should provide the repercussions. Start out with a firm objection, or a good shriek—whatever the occasion calls for. Don't bottle up your feelings—vent them! Get angry! If you don't, he'll get off on having gotten away with something. Like a kid who tries shoplifting and doesn't get caught, he'll want to see what else he can get away with.

But the kid that gets caught isn't as likely to steal again, especially if he gets caught the first time. If he doesn't get caught, he's beginning to learn that he can get away with stealing.

In the same way, if you let your husband get away with a transgression—coming home really late without calling, or inviting the in-laws without asking—you are teaching him that he can get away with that and more. You may think you're being a nice person or avoiding hassles, but you're not. You are creating much bigger problems for later.

The worse the transgression, or the longer it's been going on, the more drastic the repercussions must be.

Impossible Men

Anne, who came to one of my seminars, told me how she used shock treatment on her husband, Larry, a newspaper reporter. Larry and Anne have been married for twenty-four years, but Anne admits there were many times when she didn't think they would make it through the first ten.

"Larry's a bit of a loner," Anne said, "and a wanderer. He likes to roam wherever he wants and doesn't want to be obligated to take anyone else along if he doesn't want to." Needless to say, this caused a lot of problems in the early years of their marriage.

"I knew Larry loved me," Anne told me, "but he just wasn't ready to commit to the married lifestyle. Even when the children came along, he still acted like a single man—stopping off at the local bar for a few drinks with the guys after work, and not getting home until nine or ten. He would go off on weekend trips to follow up some lead when a phone call would have done as well. He even volunteered for assignments that took him out of the country for weeks, sometimes months. For him it was exciting, but I was stuck home with the kids. And he never consulted me.

"When I called him on it, he would look confused. He'd say something like, 'Gee, honey, that's how I make my living. You knew that when we got married. That's just me.' Of course, I nagged in the beginning, until I realized it wasn't doing a damn bit of good. It just made him want to get away more.

"About nine years into our marriage, I decided that I'd better do something drastic if I didn't want to continue being alone with two kids for the rest of my life while he took off for wherever, whenever he wanted. The kids were both in school by this time, so I went back to work as a secretary. Then one weekend when Larry took off, I turned our 'junk room' into a bedroom for myself and moved all my clothes in.

"When he got back I told him that since he wasn't sure he wanted a wife (even though I was sure he did) or a married lifestyle, we'd just be roommates from now on. He could do what he wanted without having to tell me and I could do what I wanted.

"He was stunned, of course, but went along with it because he really had no other choice. I paid for half of everything, cooked for myself and the kids, and if Larry wanted to have dinner with us, he'd have to ask for an invitation.

"The first time he tried to make love to me, I held off, telling him that if we were dating he wouldn't expect me to just leap into bed—he'd take me to dinner and a movie first! And, I wouldn't go out to dinner with him unless he called me at the office to ask for a date!

"At first, he responded by just staying out more than he had before. But I held firm. His dirty clothes were starting to pile up and his bedroom was a mess. He had to start staying home on weekends to get his clothes ready, so I'd take the kids and leave the house. I was sure he was really miserable over the whole situation, but I didn't know what his breaking point would be. It's actually quite funny what finally turned him around.

"One Saturday, trying to do his own wash, he ruined about half of his shirts. Most of his socks were already a sort of motley pinkish-gray, but for some reason, it was the shirts that did the trick. Maybe it was the idea of having to go shopping for new shirts—he really hates shopping. Or maybe it was just the final straw.

"He was waiting for me with flowers when I got home with the kids, and he actually pleaded, 'Can we please be married again?'"

That was nearly fifteen years ago, Anne told me. From that

point on, Larry started to appreciate his wife and family and to settle into normal married life. He still goes on occasional trips, but he doesn't seek out every assignment that'll take him halfway around the world. Anne and Larry are looking forward to the next twenty-four years.

If your man or your relationship has you depressed, it's for two reasons—learned helplessness and anger turned inward. Learned helplessness is the state you get into when you feel you are helpless to change your situation. Anger turned inward is what happens when we're angry with someone we love and can't bring ourselves to put the anger out there where it belongs. We feel we can't yell at him or punish him, so we begin to feel like it's our fault, that there's something wrong with us, and then we get angry at ourselves.

It's always better to express anger by taking action, before you get depressed. Taking action will help you convince your subconscious that you are not helpless to change your situation. It will also create a repercussion which may eliminate the cause of your anger.

When the Pain Is Out of Control

Is the man in your life abusive, a woman beater, a child molester, a drunk, a drug addict a gambler, a cheat?

Only you know what it's like. When he's not drunk, drugged, bullying, depressed, manic or abusive, he can be the sweetest, funniest, most adorable man in the world. That's because he's storing up points for his next binge. He'll take the trash out, bring you breakfast in bed, be wonderful, affectionate and adorable. He may even be convincingly apologetic. He'll promise never to do it again.

The problem with a perpetual abuser is that he *will* do it again—again and again. Two hours or two weeks after the last promise, your lovable man suddenly becomes totally obnoxious, crude, abusive, and definitely unlovable. Worst of all, he usually blames you for the way he is. If he can't get it up, he says it's because you weren't sexy enough. If he can't keep a job, it's because you didn't wake him for work. If he's abusive, it's because you did something wrong.

Eventually, a good relationship with him becomes impossible because you lose your self-esteem. You begin to believe it's your fault he can't make love, that you've become unlovable.

Don't ignore the problem and hope it will go away. Don't believe his promises. The longer you do nothing, the worse it gets. Let him know you won't forgive him again.

If you feel stuck with this kind of man and unable to take action, you may need help more than he does. Don't wait for him to straighten out. Get help for yourself. Keep yourself from going crazy and being dragged down with him.

Whatever you do, don't join him in his destructive behavior. Don't drink with an alcoholic, don't take drugs with a drug user. Don't figure it's easier to join him than to fight. He'll only assume you are giving your blessings to the whole operation, not that you love him so much you're willing to join in his destruction or die with him.

Is He Testing Your Love?

He may be testing you to see how far you'll let him go before you do something. Sometimes his self-destructive behavior is a test of your love to see whether you care enough to stop his destruction. If you want to save your relationship, you must take action. Find a support group that will help you, like Al-anon for families of drinkers. Next, insist that he get professional help too.

If he refuses to accept outside help, your only recourse is shock treatment. Only extraordinary shock will bring him around. Get some advice on a workable solution from an expert on your man's problem. Alcoholics Anonymous has said for years that many alcoholics only shape up when they are shocked by winding up in the gutter. Your shock treatment can have the same effect, but it must be firm, fair and predictable.

Firm means you won't change your mind.

Fair means he deserves it.

Predictable means that whenever he cheats, drinks, or becomes abusive, the repercussions will follow immediately—just as surely as night follows day.

Of course, if the problem is physical abuse, be sure that you're physically safe when he faces the repercussions you've arranged for him. If you haven't contacted the women's support group in your area, *do* so. They have good counselors and safe houses for you.

Don't say, "I know him. He won't respond to any kind of shock treatment." You'll be surprised. If the repercussions force him into a major, traumatic change of living arrangement or lifestyle, he'll respond. Most men don't like change. They like everything to stay the same, even if it means they'll have to give up getting away with something they've always been able to get away with.

Women, of course, are not immune to the same feelings. You may not like what you have, but when you imagine risking your whole relationship, possibly changing your whole life style, the thought is overwhelming. Many women choose to grin and bear it because the familiar is better than the unknown—just because they know what it's about.

In some cases, I've found that a woman is letting her man get away with something consciously and purposely because then she feels justified in doing whatever she's doing that isn't exactly kosher.

For example, one woman I counseled, a doctor's wife, admitted that she knew her husband consumed vast amounts of amphetamine to keep up with his busy practice. He was famous and worked in several hospitals. She wanted him to spend more time with her, but decided she couldn't tell him to give up the amphetamines because then she would have to give up her drinking. Be sure you really want your man to change before you consider strong medicine like shock treatment.

Shock treatment *is* an extreme way to deal with a problem in your relationship. It should be the last resort, short of leaving him. But if it's done with the intention of saving the relationship—if he knows that you love him and want him, if only he'll stop hurting you—then it's better than just walking away.

When to Save Yourself

Shock treatment doesn't always work. Sometimes the man decides he would rather continue with his unacceptable behavior, no matter what. In that case, if you can't save him, you can at least save yourself from total despair and depression. Giving him shock treatments should have helped you express your feelings, but that's probably not enough. You must have a support group run by professionals. Get professional medical, psychological or even legal help for yourself. You probably need it, and you undoubtedly deserve it.

18

Infidelity

PERHAPS the deepest hurt, the most painful pain, comes from finding out your husband is having an affair with another woman.

Womanizers

Some men are womanizers. Every woman they meet is a potential conquest. Nothing else in life is as important as their next sexual adventure. Seduction is constantly on their mind. It's as if they were reaching out for the womanness of women, not any particular woman.

"It's a sense of warmth, the female smell, the softness I seem to need," one habitual womanizer told me. "Of course, it doesn't mean I don't love my wife, or that I want to break up our marriage or would ever consider such a thing," he said. He reminded me of the old song ". . . for I'm always true to you, darling, in my fashion. . . ."

His fashion of being true, it turned out, had certain loopholes:

Out of town doesn't count.

If it furthers business, it doesn't count.

As long as it's just physical, it doesn't count.

Group sex doesn't count.

Hookers don't count.

Oral sex doesn't count.

Old girl friends don't count.

Married women don't count.

As long as you treat your wife like a queen, it doesn't count.

This guy was dead serious. These were his rules, and he lived by them. He bragged about how careful he was, and how his wife never dreamed he was unfaithful. "I kind of get off on the intrigue. Each time I'm out with another woman, I've got cover stories three layers deep. If she calls my office, for example, my secretary gives her cover story number two, and then real quick calls me. I feel like James Bond."

Sooner or later, of course, "James Bond" is going to get careless, or his elaborate cover stories will run into Murphy's Law. Then, once mutual friends know that his wife knows, the phone will ring off the hook. "Well, dear, I certainly wasn't going to be the first to tell you, but you really should know that last summer, at that big sales convention in Dallas . . ." And so on. It all comes out, and the stories seem endless. You never want to be "Mrs. Bond." This chapter will tell you how to avoid it.

I have interviewed lots of men who have had affairs while they were married. Their excuses ran the gamut, but some of the most sincere ones are:

1. Biology. Obviously, the most promiscuous men have bred the most children throughout history; the "promiscuity" gene has been passed along and has become dominant. So what's a guy to do?

2. Fantasy. From the time a little boy can read (*Playboy*, or whatever) society encourages male conquest fantasies—

fantasies of two or three beautiful blondes in a hot tub vying for us, mistress sex act fantasies, etcetera. We're programmed. So what's a guy to do?

3. Temptation. Even in the softest, most romantic tradition, it's the male who is the pursuer, the female pursued. Little boys were never programmed to say no. So now, with sexually aggressive women actually asking us to go to bed with them, what's a poor guy to do?

Outrageous? Sure, these are cheap excuses for cheating. But there's a little bit of womanizer deep inside every man. (Need I quote Jimmy Carter on the subject of Lust?) Every woman should recognize that biology, fantasy, and temptation affects her man. Preventing or stopping infidelity starts with understanding this, not denying it.

With infidelity, it is difficult to find the middle ground between denial and overreaction. Trust is one of the most important parts of marriage. When infidelity raises its ugly head, the trust is violated. Many women that I counsel were so devastated by the betrayal of their trust that they simply ended their marriages then and there. Often they are sorry, looking back with 20-20 hindsight.

Ellen, now in her mid-forties, and divorced for the past fourteen years, told me that if she had it to do over again, she wouldn't have left her husband.

"I was a fool," she sighed. "A young, arrogant fool who threw away a perfectly charming, wonderful, successful man for a moment's angry pride."

Nick and Ellen had lived together two years before they were married. They were married three years and had just had a beautiful baby girl they both adored when everything fell apart for Ellen.

Nick, a handsome musician, traveled with a rock 'n' roll band. "I found out about a couple of wild weekends he'd had on the road and when he came home, I ordered him out of the house, shouting that I was going to call my lawyer first thing in the morning," Ellen recalled.

Nick pleaded and even cried, begging Ellen to forgive him, promising it would never happen again. But Ellen was so hurt, she sneered at his love. "I knew he loved me and I loved him, but I thought what he'd done was contemptible. The more he begged me to forgive him, the more superior I felt. I was right and he was wrong. It was all black and white. No grays in those days. He had cheated and I was going to punish him. Now I realize I was really punishing myself too.

"But then, I wanted him to suffer. I wanted to hurt his heart as much as he had hurt mine. I wanted him to lose the ones he loved, me and his daughter. It was the only way I knew to get back at him.

"I had tried to be so perfect, I had loved him so much more than anybody else in the world. And I was pretty. I had such a good figure. I cooked for him. I adored him. All I could think of was getting even because I was so hurt. I deliberately wrecked my life."

Nick and Ellen got divorced. It was a long, drawn-out, messy affair. "Nick was stubborn and he kept refusing to believe that I would actually go through with it. I had to prove to him that I was tougher than he was. I signed the divorce papers but he never did. I guess that means I'm divorced and he isn't."

Since Nick and Ellen have a little girl, they've kept in touch over the years. Ellen has perhaps suffered more for her impetuous revenge than Nick. She has moved many times and struggled to make ends meet as a single mother. Nick, on the other hand, has been able to live the same fabulous lifestyle he always did.

"A few years ago we were all three sitting around looking at the family albums," Ellen told me. "Nick said to me, 'What happened to us, Ellie?' as we both looked at a picture of the two of us, so young and obviously in love. I think I felt a greater sense of loss at that moment than I had years before when I signed the divorce papers."

Ellen says she doesn't think about marriage anymore. "I haven't met a man that makes me feel even remotely like Nick did, and I won't settle for anything less than that. Besides, I've been alone a long time and I guess I'm getting used to it." She sighed.

Although there was a time when a single indiscretion was grounds for immediate divorce, that is no longer the case. Many a woman whose husband has had an affair more serious than Nick's has forgiven him and gone on to rebuild trust and an enduring marriage.

Why Is It Always the Woman's Problem?

Unlike our grandparents, we don't seem to have years to develop communication and understanding in a marriage. In today's fast-track world, we expect instant, full happiness from a marriage. Perhaps for this reason, many marriages break up in the first years. If it isn't working, we begin to look around. Sex outside of marriage is offered everywhere. Divorce is all around us. It strikes roughly 50 percent of all marriages today. No-fault divorces seem easy.

To stay married, we women must take the initiative to develop fuller understanding and more effective communication—and we must be fiercely protective of our relationships. Divorce is generally not an acceptable alternative. We women have worked hard for our families. They are the center of our lives. Also, our standard of living usually depends on staying married. Divorce will drastically lower an ex-wife's standard of living; the ex-husband's standard of living usually continues to rise.

There is no advantage to separating. We must learn to keep our marriages intact. With thousands of sexy single women out there moaning that all the good ones are taken, and ready to snatch up any unhappy husband, the ball is in our court. We can keep our men from even thinking about straying, by making them feel understood in a special way.

Every marriage is different. Whether or not you iron polyester shirts is up to you. We all decide what things we will or won't do for our mates. The important thing, though, is making sure that what we're doing is something he wants. That way, he's already more inclined and primed to do something we want.

I'll never forget Robin and Hank. They were the traditional perfect couple. Robin was the perfect wife, a woman I often looked at with envy when I was single. She seemed to have it all—all the advantages of a terrific career, a wonderful husband and great kids as well. How do some people get so lucky? I used to wonder.

Everything about her was faultless, her nails, her figure, her clothes, her hair, her kids, her house. Married twelve years, Robin and Hank had two perfectly beautiful children, a boy, 7, and a girl, 6. Robin had a string of high-paying jobs in advertising art, and her services were always in demand. Because Hank traveled a lot in his job as a sound engineer for movies, Robin took care of everything at home.

Bills, kids, gardening, cleaning, taxes, social obligations, she did it all for him. He never had to worry about the details of life—all he had to do was make movie stars sound good. Their friends in the industry looked to Robin and Hank as a model of stability and reliability. Imagine how shocked everyone was when Hank moved out. And, yes, there was another woman.

Robin, ever practical, always in charge, couldn't believe her rational, reliable Hank was shacking up with another woman. She firmly believed he would come to his senses, so she refused to do anything. "He can't just leave me and the kids. I know he'll be back," she cried. "He's just not the type to run off with some Bimbo." Robin couldn't believe it was really happening. After all, hadn't they waited five years to have kids to make sure their relationship was stable? He'd be back. They belonged together.

He didn't come back. He just kept running away from his perfect wife, from woman to woman. They weren't as pretty, or as perfect, or as helpful with his life, but they did something more important—they gave him what he really needed. They listened to him; they needed him.

Poor Robin. She thought that as long as she did everything a wife is supposed to do and whatever else she could think of as well, that Hank would be happy.

Poor Hank. He felt overwhelmed by Robin. He said he never had a chance to make decisions for himself, to balance his own checkbook or buy a houseplant or underwear or a shirt. He never picked a repairman or decided what to buy at the grocery store. Robin took care of everything.

It wasn't until Robin and I had replayed her and Hank's situation several times that Robin began to understand. At first she was too hurt to try.

The woman Hank had first moved in with was a rather plain and overweight single mother with two kids living in a one-bedroom apartment. "How could he leave our beautiful home and our children and go live like that with her kids?"

And it was true. Their Hollywood hilltop home was magnificent, and the new woman in Hank's life was dowdy next to Robin. But Hank was getting what he wanted, someone to talk to, someone to ask his advice, someone to let him be in charge.

No matter how perfect Robin became, she had never related to Hank in the way he thought was important. It's true that some women are born with a special way of getting close to men, but Robin had to learn. From her perspective, everything looked perfect. From Hank's, it didn't.

Hank and Robin were different in some important ways. Hank was auditory, and Robin was visual.

Throughout her life, Robin saw things in pictures. How things looked was most important to her. Her life was a study in neat and perfect images both at home and in her work. She really believed that making everything look right would keep Hank happy, since it kept her happy.

Not so. Hank was a hearing person, and all of Robin's efforts to have everything look right were lost on him. Worse, her bustling around to get everything done kept her on a totally different wavelength from his.

Hank needed more talk, less action, but in Robin's busy schedule to keep things perfect, there just had never been time. He needed to talk things over quietly and be consulted on decisions. He wanted to hear certain words from Robin in a tone of voice that would make him feel loved. What Hank felt, but couldn't quite articulate, was the need to share his life on an auditory level.

"I let it go on so long, it was too late to talk about all the things in our life that were wrong. It was nothing in particular, just everything. We just never communicated," he said afterwards.

When Hank found another woman, probably more auditory, with more time to give to him, he suddenly began to blossom and feel really needed and loved.

Over and over again, women have asked me, "Why do some men make the kind of deep commitment that they never break, the kind of love and devotion our grandparents had? How come we find it so hard to get those feelings from the men in our lives?"

By now you've seen that a man who feels special stays around. Women who have used my techniques to make a man fall in love with them, and then kept using those techniques to strengthen that love, have succeeded in keeping their husbands very happy—and very faithful.

Not all married women have had the advantage of these love techniques, though. Many, many marriages today are threatened by infidelity. Every wife should learn how to spot it, and how to deal with it.

Ten Terrible Times to Suspect He's Cheating

1. When he no longer wants sex

2. When he suddenly has to work late and has all kinds of new obligations that take him away from home

3. When he gets mysterious phone calls

4. When he arrives home smelling faintly of another woman

5. When he arrives home and washes feverishly

6. When he has unfamiliar colored hairs on his clothes

7. When he gets too nice, too suddenly

8. When he gets dressed up to "go fishing"

9. When his routine changes with no believable reason

10. When he forgets the carpool, can't remember the dog's name, and you have to tell him everything three times

How to Find Out for Sure
(From Some Who've Caught the Cad)

Smell him (and the car) for strange perfume.
Make love soon after he gets home
Follow up on any hints from friends
If a working-late story sounds fishy, create a sudden cat/dog/kid "emergency" so you need to reach him.
If you suspect he's dashing out to the corner store to make phone calls, follow him discreetly to find out.
If you're quite sure, confront him. Do it immediately. Don't wait until you catch him in the act. Don't pretend you didn't notice. Confront him right away. The longer you wait, the longer he'll keep screwing around and thinking it's okay. Like the kid who doesn't get caught shoplifting, he'll quickly learn he is above the "domestic laws" of faithfulness. He'll get habituated to the mistress in his life, and he'll start to enjoy having gotten away with something—adding secondary thrills to the primary ones.

How to Confront a Philanderer

The way to confront him is to let him know you're concerned for your marriage. Tell him it's not him you don't trust,
it's all those women out there, so you want to know where he is
when he's out. He may bluster and bluff, but just show quiet
determination. Tell him the more he resists your request, the
more worried you are; you love him, and you're going to protect your marriage like a tiger.

If he agrees to letting you know his whereabouts, the battle
is half won. If he 'fesses up to some indiscretion and seems
genuinely sincere about it, the battle is three-quarters won. On
the other hand, if he acts like a cornered rat and says "Well, I
don't want a marriage where I'm going to be suffocated," or
something similar, you *know*.

What to Do When You Know for
Sure He's Been Unfaithful

These "tough love" rules were compiled by analyzing
women who were able to curtail their philandering mates. The
rules also were corroborated by divorced, cheating hubbies
who told me that if their wives had done the following, their
marriages would have been saved.

Remember the principle of shock treatment (chapter 17)?
The repercussions he suffers from continuing his Don Juan
ways must be worse than the trauma of ending them.

If he doesn't admit he's cheating, but you're sure he is,
apply pressure anywhere you can. Call all your mutual friends
and tell them you think he's fooling around and ask for their
help. This will immediately cut off his source of excuses and
friends who are covering for him. They will be very uncomfortable and most will talk to him about your call.

Let him get a few buddy-to-buddy talks from his priest, co-workers, old pals and relatives. Tell his mother. Insist that you and he go for marriage counseling. Put him under immediate, overwhelming pressure to explain what's going on and to clean up his act.

Whether he admits he's cheating or not, insist he stop immediately. Let him know in no uncertain terms that you are very, very upset. Show him. Sound a little crazy. Threaten to find and shoot the woman. Let him know he's risking his family and his marriage. Run down the possible outcomes—alienating the children and contracting a sexual disease are good ones to point out. Let him know he's facing severe lifelong financial damages, no rest, no peace, as long as "she" is in his life.

Make it really uncomfortable—if not impossible—for him to continue meeting the other woman. Peer pressure combined with his fear of loss may very well help your cause. The idea is for him to conclude that cutting off the affair is easier than continuing, that no nooky is worth the aggravation he's going to have or what it's going to cost.

And don't stop with him. If you can track down the other woman, call her. She may not even know he's married. Write letters to her. If she admits to having the affair with him but is defiant, write her employer. Write her landlady. Make it so uncomfortable for her that she slams the door in his face next time he visits.

One "other woman" told me she cut off her married lover when his wife showed up at her door in the rain with three small children in tow. Sure, the other woman's a "bimbo," but she may have a conscience. You can make the affair more trouble than it's worth, for both of them.

Sound like overkill? I don't believe so. We're talking about the survival of your marriage. There is no threat to a marriage like another woman. Even if he's not likely to run off with the bimbo of the moment, she's driving a wedge between you and your husband. His energy, interest and love are being siphoned off. Your trust is shattered, your future is up in the air, and you are depressed.

Even if you can pull yourself together to use the love techniques in this book, what good are they if your man is never around? You have every right to be protective of your marriage, and you must fight for it like a tigress. If you do, you will only garner respect. His friends will respect you and secretly admire him, for having a wife so willing to fight for him. After the initial shock, he will probably reach the same conclusions.

Typically, philandering husbands told me, "If she had caught me early enough, before I realized it was so easy, I would have stopped." And, "I guess if she had found out and gotten my parents on my back or threatened me with divorce or disgrace or something before I got so good at lying to her, I would have stopped."

Almost every man who has been unfaithful told me the same thing. If there were repercussions the first time he did it, he wouldn't have done it again. If you catch him down the line—a third or fourth affair—immediate repercussions are even more important.

While I was researching a book about a very rich man and the many mistresses he kept simultaneously, I asked him, "How did you get so many?" He told me, "I thought something awful would happen if I took a mistress, but I did it and nothing terrible happened. So I took another one, and still nothing happened. So now I have seven." He smiled like the cat that swallowed the canary. Because he was able to find women who would go along with the program, he just kept adding more and more.

Jeanette, 52, and married for twenty-seven years to Ralph, was totally distraught when she came to me for counseling. Ralph, it seemed, had been fooling around for many years. "He was always looking for a new conquest, even when I was pregnant with our daughter," she told me. She wasn't even sure he had ever been faithful to her for more than a couple of months between affairs.

"But things are really bad now," she wept. "He moved out last month and got an apartment at a swinging singles complex where he has all the women he wants. He said he needed some 'space.'"

Jeanette still had most of Ralph's clothes, his African artifact collection left over from his import-export business, and all his junk mail. "I'm afraid to even think about a divorce or anything because then I'd lose everything—my home, all the property we've accumulated—it's all in his name. Besides, he spends part of his time here, and I keep hoping he'll move back."

Because she had let him get away with treating her like a second-class wife, with frequent affairs over the years, Ralph was totally spoiled. He knew without a doubt that he could do whatever he wanted and Jeanette would still be grateful whenever he stopped by, and even cook him dinner!

"Why not change the locks on the house, pack his clothes, and put them outside in boxes? Tell him he can come back when he cleans up his act and not before," I counseled Jeanette.

"Oh no," she wailed. "If I did that then he would leave me and I'd lose everything."

Eventually Jeanette came to realize what she was doing. By letting Ralph get away with his outrageous behavior, she was giving her silent consent to it.

Ralph's habitual philandering was not the kind of behavior that could be cured by just telling him he couldn't do those things anymore. He had learned long ago that what Jeanette said didn't mean a thing. He could sweet talk or scare her out of it in a minute. What he didn't know was that Jeanette was learning new ways to modify his behavior. She discovered that in order to straighten Ralph's bent twig she would have to bend it as far as possible in the other direction.

Since Jeanette's words never meant anything to Ralph, she realized she would have to take drastic action, real shock treatment. One weekend when she knew he was going to be out of town, she did lock him out.

Ralph was furious. He carried on about how all his business papers were in the house and he couldn't take care of their property without them, but Jeanette simply took every document she could find to a tough divorce lawyer, who wrote a very strong letter to Ralph at his new address.

It took less than one week for Ralph to come to his senses. He suddenly realized he could lose a lot and that Jeanette wasn't afraid of him anymore. Her shock treatment turned him around, because it was out of her usual pattern.

Instead of trying to talk Ralph out of his rotten behavior, Jeanette took action for the first time. She showed Ralph she would no longer be bullied by him. That was over two years ago. Since then, Ralph has seemed almost relieved to be monogamously settled in with Jeanette, and fascinated with the new, assertive side of his wife.

But actually, Jeanette was lucky that the shock treatment worked. She had really let Ralph's outrageous cheating go on far too long, to the point where they were in fact estranged without a legal separation. Never let infidelity go that long.

You must absolutely put a stop to his lying, sneaking, cheating behavior before he gets used to having his cake and eating it too. You have to let him know you won't put up with infidelity before it becomes a pattern. You have to provide repercussions that will stop him before he gets used to cheating and before he begins to get secondary thrills from having pulled something on you. If he insists on continuing the affair, you will know you've done everything possible to stop it. You'll feel better about yourself.

The Dangerous Game of Getting Even

There is one kind of repercussion which I cannot recommend—"getting even." "If it's fair for him, it's fair for me" sounds vaguely equitable, but it misses the point. It's *not* fair for either of you, or for your marriage. Two wrongs don't make a right. If you're both cheating, your relationship is in a downward spiral.

What if you don't consider infidelity "wrong"? What if fidelity was never promised? As a single woman in the sixties, I had very closeup exposure to "open" relationships, "group" marriages, and other experimental forms of coupling. I certainly make no moral judgment on people who enter willingly into nontraditional relationships. They just rarely work out, that's all.

It may be different in other cultures, but in Western society today, a monogamous man-woman relationship seems to work best. Our world is full of uncertainty, change, and stress. Kids seem to need a Mommy and Daddy more than they ever have. A man and a woman can cope better if they can trust the other to be there, if they can function as a team.

If you have a good relationship, and you're both playing around because you think it's the sophisticated thing to do, or you're both cheating to "stay even," you're playing a very dangerous game.

Twelve Infidelity Survival Tips You Can Count On

1. Don't ignore the obvious in the hopes that it will go away.

2. Remember, his being "best friends" with another woman is as dangerous as sex. Maybe more so. *You* should always be his best friend.

3. If it makes you feel better, diet, work out, get sexier or prettier. But don't think you're going to diet him back or seduce him back. Sure, he'll go to bed with you, but he'll still go back to her, unless you take action.

4. When he comes home early, be nice. When he stays out late, let him feel your ire.

5. Whatever happens, don't let him see that you're depressed. Nothing drives a man away faster than a depressed woman. Let him think you're happy without him. He'll be intrigued and much more likely to come back. Men avoid depressed women and are drawn to happy ones. Let your women friends and counselor help with your depression.

6. Beware of "neurotic stimulus generalization." That means that because your husband is bad, you decide that everything is bad—the kids, your life, the rotten world. This will make you even more miserable. Make a list of everything that's right with you. Keep it handy.

7. Don't blame yourself. Keep your anger focused where it belongs—on him and the "bimbo." (The other woman is always a "bimbo"—or worse!) Remember, anger turned inward causes depression.

8. Don't make it easy for him to move out. Possession is nine-tenths of the law. Don't let him take even his toothbrush to her house.

9. Fight. You have more to fight for than the other woman.

10. Remember, an overwhelming show of force on your part will stop him. Ultimately he'll be flattered by it.

11. Break your pattern. Do something unexpected. Let him know he doesn't have you totally pegged, that there's still a little mystery, a you he hasn't even imagined. Be outrageous!

12. Invoke all your anchors from the past: loving pictures, gifts you gave each other, favorite songs, foods, and scents. Be cool. Don't point them out. Let them work on his unconscious.

When You're Tempted

A stranger with a certain look in his eye looks at you in a certain way and you know, if you wanted to, you could have an affair.

Someone you've always admired and respected suddenly puts his arm around you in a "different" way, and you know the invitation has been made. He talks to you with an intimacy that says, "I'm really interested in you. I'm really listening to you. I really care about what you say."

You don't mean to have an affair. You love your husband. It's just that lately he hasn't been as attentive, as affectionate, as adoring as he used to be. You wonder if you're still attractive. You want romance in your life.

Most women who have affairs do it by accident. They don't plan to, it just happens. Of all married couples, 75 percent of the men and 50 percent of the women will have sex outside of marriage. Many of them will stay married. The affair will almost inevitably hurt the marriage, in some way. Some couples will split up. Most of the ones who split up will be sorry.

AVOIDING TEMPTATION

Make it standard practice to let people know you're married. Always do it right away. That way you don't give yourself time to develop an "innocent" little interest in whoever he is—the cute door-to-door insurance salesman or the new vice president at work. Always speak pridefully of your hubby (even if he wasn't so lovable this morning); people will respect you for it, and you'll keep yourself away from temptation.

Don't flirt. Because women usually ignore men who flirt with them, they fail to realize that it's different the other way around. A man considers a flirtatious stare from a woman as a serious invitation. If he's a creep, he'll start following you, or worse. If he's quite charming, a flirt can lead to a chat, which can lead to a drink, which can lead to a ride home, which can lead to . . . Is this really what you want?

IF YOU'VE AVOIDED HIM
BUT YOU'RE STILL TEMPTED

Remind yourself of this: Once you start an affair, it either gets better or worse. If it gets worse, you'll feel degraded and sick with yourself for taking the risk of getting caught; if it gets better, you're going to want to be with him all the time. . . . You're not starting something you can control, despite all the articles in women's magazines. If you want to stay married, don't start an affair, no matter how much you're tempted.

If the man tempting you is ready to have an affair with a married woman, he's no virgin. Think about how many partners this guy has probably been with (believe *nothing* of what he tells you), and think long and hard about what you might catch from him.

IF YOU'RE ALREADY HAVING AN AFFAIR

Don't fall insanely, obsessively in love. Falling in love makes you act weird. People at home will notice the changes.

End it. But not by calling the guy from home. Telephone bills tell tales. Eavesdropping kids tell tales.

If you don't want to break up your marriage, don't tell anyone about your affair. Not your best friend, not your mother, and especially not your husband—no matter what he has said about not being jealous. And not even if you suspect he's having one, too. Mild-mannered, otherwise rational husbands can go totally berserk over a wife's infidelity.

The reason that many marriages break up when the woman has an affair is that we women seem driven to tell. Unlike men who cheat, we get caught because we tell on ourselves. I remember one friend I accidentally caught out with a man other than her husband. Naturally, I never told. But she did. When I asked her why she told her husband, she said, "I wanted to get even. I wanted to let him know I was still desirable." Dumb. *Don't* try to get even. If you feel guilty, don't dump it on your husband. If you can't live with your guilt, see a clergyman or a shrink. Whatever you do, don't tell your husband.

IF YOU GET CAUGHT

Deny everything.
Plead temporary insanity.
Swear nothing happened and it'll never happen again.
Tell him you love him.

Keeping Love Alive

LOTS of men and women fall in love, get married, and stay together for the rest of their lives. You can use their secrets to keep your own relationship together.

Who are those loving couples and how have they stayed together and in love so long? You'll meet some of them in this chapter and discover their most powerful tool for keeping love alive—love triggers.

Love Triggers

Love triggers are anything that will trigger the memory of the loving feelings you have shared together. Over the years, many women tell me they have developed lots of little reminders of the shared history they have with their husbands. Then, when something goes wrong, or just isn't as good as it has been, they pull out their love triggers and the men get all romantic.

Love triggers can be things, like letters or pictures or mementos. Len, a writer, and Rita, an art director, have been married for thirty-five years. They have four grown sons, three grandchildren, and are as much in love today as they were when they were teenagers. They both use a special love trigger:

"We married right out of high school," Rita told me, "and two years later our first son was born.

"Len was drafted when the baby was just learning to walk and by that time I was pregnant with our second son. I moved near the base to be with Len for the first few months, but then he was sent to Korea and I was left alone with a toddler and another baby on the way.

"It was tough on both of us with him so far away and neither of us being able to telephone the other. So we wrote letters, long passionate letters filled with our love for one another and our hopes for the future. We wrote about our plans for when Len was discharged. We decided on the new baby's name through our letters and discussed where we would live when Len was home again.

"We put everything that happened to either of us in our letters. Even though we had known one another since we were kids, we discovered so many new things through our letters, and I think we wrote things that were so personal we would never have talked about them."

Len was gone four years. When he got home, Rita told me it was like a second honeymoon.

"I grew closer to our boys, seeing them through Len's eyes. Since I went to work right after they were born, I had missed a lot of their growing. Sharing the skills they learned with Len was wonderful. Of course, we had fights. Who doesn't?

"But whenever Len would get cranky with me or distant or start to take me for granted, I'd simply take out the box of letters he had written me from Korea and quietly lay them in his lap and leave the room. The first time I did that, he just sat there for over an hour, reading each letter until tears were running down his cheeks. 'I meant every word,' he told me, 'and I mean them now. Thanks for reminding me.'

"Now he pulls the same thing on me when I get upset. If I'm nagging him or sniping at something, he takes out the letters I wrote to him and hands them to me.

"One time he said, 'Here, read these, honey, and see if you

can learn something. They were written by a beautiful lady I had a passionate love affair with during the war. Now she knew how to talk to a man.' Of course they were my letters."

Sandy, a lawyer, and Jeff, a dentist, married seventeen years with three children, also have a love trigger.

"When we were married, Jeff gave me a gold charm bracelet," she told me. "Each time something significant in our life happens, he gives me a new charm. I have a charm for each anniversary, each child's birth, our first house, trips we've taken together, even a charm to represent my passing the bar.

"Whenever I need to cheer us up, I just get out the bracelet and put it on. After all these years, I think Jeff smiles when he hears the charms jangle because he knows all the happiness they represent. Sometimes we sit together on the couch and go through the charms, reading what each one says on the back and remembering each and every occasion. We always wind up misty-eyed and feeling very warm and close."

The artist Chagall used a love trigger when he was broke and courting the love of his life. He took her a bouquet of flowers every day. The floral bouquet became a symbol of their great love and can be seen in almost all of his paintings.

Think about your own relationship. Perhaps you have love triggers you aren't even aware of, or haven't used lately. If your husband is a visual type, flowers, pictures, love letters, dressing in special clothes, even a particular view could be a love trigger for him. If he's auditory, try special music, or pet names, or special things you say to each other. If he's a feelings man, try a special touch, a particular fabric, a soft velvet or fluffy fur, or even a favorite food that always makes him feel loved.

Love triggers are powerful. They allow you to control your relationship in a way you couldn't without them. Triggers reach to a deep, unconscious psychological level. They go beyond words because they make your partner feel the loving feelings he had before.

Sex Triggers

A smell can be a sexual trigger. Many men report being turned on by real body odors more than by perfume. Other men have a favorite scent that excites them.

If you don't have a scent trigger, get one. Then use that same perfume each time you are making love. Sprinkle it liberally on the sheets, in your bath water. Buy candles for your bedroom in the same scent. Then, you won't even have to be around and your husband will be turned on just smelling your particular scent trigger. And after a while, all you have to do is put the perfume on, and he's ready for action. The scent trigger you planted works for you without your having to say or do anything, except put on some perfume.

Whenever my husband goes on a trip out of town, I spray a little of my cologne on the inside fabric of his suitcase, some on his slippers. It helps keep everything smelling nice, and I know he'll be thinking of me, even when he's thousands of miles away.

One woman who came to me for consultation about her husband decided to use Joy Jell and Emotion Lotion to get her feelings husband to enjoy sex more. Each time they made love, she brought out a bottle of their favorite sex prop. "I told him I couldn't decide which flavor I liked, so I bought a lot of different ones, and we were going to pick our favorite," she told me.

"The directions said to rub it in and blow on it. So I started with the strawberry flavor. First, I rubbed it all over both my hands, then I put a little on one of his nipples, and then I put some on one of mine. Gently I rubbed it in, and then I blew on it. It got hot, and I said, sort of matter of factly, 'Well, that's the strawberry. I'll taste yours, then you taste mine,' and licked his nipple with the tip of my tongue.

'Your turn,' I said, and he was already showing more interest than I had seen in a long time, in spite of lots of other things I'd tried. He kissed my breast, really tenderly.

"'Not bad,' he said of the taste test. And we both sat there licking our lips. Then I said, 'Now, let's taste the grape. I'll put it on your other nipple, and mine too.'

"By the time we got to the cherry flavor, I could see that I couldn't drag the tasting out much longer. Jokingly, I told him, 'How about a little cherry where there hasn't been any in a long time?' And I put the cherry-flavored jell on his penis. I rubbed it slowly up and down and didn't stop until he was hard. He kissed me and we shared the taste of grape and strawberry and cherry. It was wonderful.

"Afterwards we went out for ice cream. 'I think I'll have strawberry,' I said innocently, testing to see how well the trigger was going to work. I could see that look in his eye. I knew I had done well.

"Now, whenever I want him to be sexy, I just bring out something fruit flavored. Strawberry jam makes him feel sexy, grapes excite him, even coconut suntan oil has become a sex symbol. If we're out somewhere, we can talk about making a little fruit salad when we go home, or over the weekend, and nobody but us knows what we're really talking about."

Memories that Keep Love Glowing

Almost every couple I've ever talked to who has been to-gether more than a few years can cite having survived at least one terrible trauma. No matter whether they've living together or married, they report surviving financial problems, being broke, being in a business together and having it fail, losing jobs, losing all their savings in an investment scheme, and even being robbed of everything they owned.

Other couples report surviving tragedies like the death of a child, a lingering illness of one partner or the other, children with terrible problems, and even long-term separations where a partner has gone to jail. Almost every long-time married couple has a story of when they came very close to splitting up.

Many have even split temporarily but have survived affairs and enormous changes in lifestyles both up and down. And then there are the couples who haven't survived these traumas of everyday living.

How are the survivors different? They are bonded by their experiences and their memories. The memories of when things were better, the beautiful, happy times they've had together and even the memory of having survived the bad times.

Of all the couples I talked to in my research, I was most impressed by Bob and Alberta. Their most shining example of married love is one I'll never forget.

Bob and Alberta had just celebrated their seventy-third wedding anniversary when I interviewed them on their farm in Washington. Bob, 93, and Alberta, 90, have nine children, nineteen grandchildren and ten great-grandchildren.

Bob is mostly the silent type, but you can tell how much he adores Alberta. He's always touching her, hugging her, sneaking up and planting a kiss on her, even pinching her in the rear. Sometimes their kids are a little embarrassed by the lovey-dovey old folks, but I found myself wanting to make sure my husband and I stayed that excited and interested in each other when we're that old, so I listened carefully to Alberta's story.

"Our love was put to the test many times," she told me. "We went through the Depression together with four little children and no work to be found. Finally, we were forced to leave our farm in Oklahoma because of the dust storms and the long drought. We moved to Washington State with barely enough money to buy a decent meal.

"Most men would have panicked, but not my Bobby. He just tightened his belt and set about finding a job and working toward buying us another home. Women didn't have careers in those days, so I made my role as homemaker my career. I was determined to be the best there was.

"Bobby didn't have to lift a finger when he came home from work, and I liked it that way. He worked long, hard hours digging and hauling, and making him happy was my job. I loved it and I know he respected me for it. He never took me for granted and he always treated me as if I was still his best girl."

Eventually, they bought a new farm, but life still wasn't easy. "With nine kids we didn't have a lot left over, but at least we could grow our food. It was hard for us to be alone, but Bobby didn't let that stop him from courting his girl, as he used to say.

"We couldn't afford to go anywhere, but we had a big farm and built-in baby-sitters with the older kids. We'd tell them we'd have to go out and sow, and then we'd go for long walks on our land. We'd picnic under our favorite oak tree near the Yakima River. And we'd make love there, giggling and whispering about what we'd do if the kids ever found us naked. They never did." Alberta's youngest daughter, 48 and divorced, told me she never knew until right then that's what her parents had been doing in the field all those times.

As they got older, and the ground got harder, and there got to be more money, Alberta and Bob would drive to the next town and check into a motel for a few hours, just to get away. "We'd get all excited. Just the way the desk clerk would look at us with no luggage and holding hands would get us all warm. In those days, doing something like that was rather naughty, and that made it even more fun.

"The next day, I'd always find a huge bouquet of flowers on the dresser when I woke up. Bob picked them himself and there was always a note with the flowers. I saved the notes over the years, and whenever things were bad and one of the kids was sick or the crops failed, I'd bring out the notes he sent me with the flowers and we'd sit and read them together, and we'd always feel better."

Even today, with both Bob and Alberta in their nineties, they are so obviously in love that their children admit to being jealous, and curious about how they stay that way. Alberta let us in on her secrets one afternoon when Bob was out.

"I always let him know he's still the sexiest, most handsome

man I've ever known," Alberta told me and two of her daugh-
ters, as we sat in her real country kitchen. "I'm jealous. And I
let him know it. It's a sort of joke with us. At parties I'll pick out
the most beautiful girl in the room and then whisper to Bob,
'That little blond hussy is flirting with you, honey. Don't you
dare let me catch you looking at her or there'll be hell to pay
when I get you home!'

"Actually, we both know the young lady wasn't flirting with
him, but it does his ego good to think that maybe she could be."

Bob and Alberta's day is filled with lots of long hugs, hand
squeezes and romantic cuddling. "It's cute; we think it's neat,"
say their grandchildren, even if Bob and Alberta's children
think they're really an anomaly in today's world. In spite of
that, several of Bob and Alberta's children confessed that they
always compare their marriages to their parents' and often find
them lacking. They wonder what it is their mother and father
do that they don't do, how they kept their love alive through
years of struggle. Alberta reminisced about how they stayed in
love.

"Life has a way of sobering people up sometimes, but we
stay young because we both have a good sense of humor.
There've been times when I've been out of sorts about something, and I'll be doing the dishes and grumbling about something, and Bob will pop me on the rear with a dish towel and
say something like, 'Your rear's as sassy as your tongue, honey-
bee.'

"We're still very passionate," Alberta assured me. "Bob
kisses me just the way he did when we were young. We hold
hands when we walk down the street or when we just sit on the
sofa watching television.

"We touch a lot. A squeeze of a hand can do so much to
cheer a person up or just let them know you're there and you
love them."

Alberta and Bob are both natural experts at anchoring
(chapter 12) and triggering love's memories.

If you don't have any terrific peak love experiences with

your mate, you may want to invent one. As I mentioned in an earlier chapter, I was once writing a story about one of the richest men in the world and his many mistresses. On visiting them, I was curious to find out how they all kept him interested.

I found out that they invented holidays to celebrate with him. He would have a half-birthday, an anniversary of the day each met him, the day they took their first trip together, and annual parties for his new car—just about anything they could think of. And, of course, there were always lots of photographs to be shared.

But the most ingenious romantic memory I ever heard about was created by Diane, a bank manager, for her and husband Frank's tenth anniversary. They had been married seventeen years when I talked to them about how they kept their love alive:

"Our love life had gotten a little predictable," Diane told me one evening as we all sat on the porch of their ranch-style home in Malibu, overlooking the California coast. "I wanted to give Frank a super wedding anniversary gift, something wild and romantic that he'd always remember. We had just moved in and we loved the beach so much, I wanted to make it a real part of our lives."

"She had everything planned," Frank told me. "We had just gotten our dream house here at the beach. I got home from work and there were clothes laid out on the bed, a note telling me to put them on, and a map, showing me where to go.

"It read like a treasure map. Turn left at the large boulder, walk toward the small clump of trees on your right, take fifteen paces past the trees, turn right behind the sand cove—or something like that.

"Anyway, I followed her instructions exactly, and when I came to the spot, there she sat in full evening dress. She was wearing this long black velvet strapless gown. It had a slit up one side and she had one of her long legs sticking out almost indecently. She had taken our card table out and set it up on the beach with a satin tablecloth and our best china and silver and crystal wine goblets.

"There was champagne chilling in a silver ice bucket and a portable stereo with our favorite music playing. The ocean was pounding and crashing against the shore, the sun was setting, and the gulls screamed at us. It was the most exciting moment of my life. She was exquisite. I'll never forget it." He grinned. "That alone would keep me in love with her forever.

"Then while my heart is pounding and I'm standing there like a dummy with my mouth hanging open looking at her thighs and cleavage, she puts on this Gloria Swanson voice and says, 'Happy Anniversary, darling,' and pours the champagne. It was the most incredible moment.

"We talked for hours just about everything and we laughed and drank champagne and ate cold Cornish game hens stuffed with wild rice and grapes and listened to the sound of the surf and the music on the radio. We held hands. It was magical."

Later, Diane told me, "I think we fell in love all over again that night. We made love on the beach in a small sheltered cove on the satin tablecloth. We didn't undress. He just pushed up my skirt and unzipped his trousers. It was a public beach and we were both worried about being caught, but it was exciting.

"Now we have a tradition. Each year on our anniversary we do something wild and crazy, something so romantic that we're both blown away by it. One year we went to a hotel and stayed in the jungle suite where the walls look like they're carved from rough stone and the floors and bed are covered with thick, dark fur. All the furniture is heavy and rugged. Another time we stayed in the cupid room, where everything is pink and red and there's this big golden cupid hanging over your heart-shaped bed. We've been on an overnight cruise and even went to an X-rated motel once. We look forward to our anniversaries more and more each year. We plan for them all year, deciding where to go and what to do, and then we remember them for a long time afterwards."

If you don't have some kind of romantic triggers, now's the time to develop some. Then they'll be there when you need them.

Romantic Memories and a History Together

The romantic memories and the history you share together are the things that hold you together in times of trouble. The laughter you've shared, the tears you've cried, the times you've been there for each other, all make up your romantic history. To keep your relationship romantic, you must keep building a romantic history together.

Don't just settle into a daily grind where one day follows another without any memorable moments. Create them. Plan things to do together that you can talk about afterwards . . . memorable and unusual foods you share . . . places you visit together . . . experiences you have.

Some women in my groups have put new fun in their marriages by taking their husbands on erotic explorations of neighborhood sex shops, by reading from sexy books together, and by acting out sexual fantasies. Even when the fantasy doesn't work out, the evening leaves something to remember afterwards, they all agreed.

One couple decided to try a bondage fantasy. "He was going to tie my feet together and then rape me," she said. "I burst out laughing. To this day we joke about it."

Triggers in His Love Language

When you decide to create a love trigger, one of those beautiful, subtle reminders of how much he loves you, do it in his Love Language. For instance, if your man is a visual man, you'll want a trigger he can see. A photo album, a framed picture, a bouquet of flowers (both visual- and feelings-inspiring), a romantic view, a favorite book, a video tape of a favorite movie, are all good visual triggers.

If your man is auditory, you will want to develop triggers that make sounds. A special way you say his name, a pet name, a special song or a favorite singer, an album you both love, a concert, a taped special message from you on his birthday or your anniversary are good triggers.

If your man is a feelings man, your triggers should stimulate his sense of touch, taste, smell, or psychological comfort. For example, he would respond to a particular perfume, special fabrics, satin sheets or pillowcases, the aroma of his favorite dish cooking, foods you love to share, even special places you go to that have spiritual meaning to you both.

Learn a new skill together, take lessons, share your accomplishments. One couple I counseled took dancing lessons. Each time they practiced together it was a shared romantic moment, a history created with each new dance learned. Afterwards, they went different places to dance, on a cruise ship, to conventions and parties. Dancing opened a whole new world to them.

Another couple joined Toastmasters and practiced public speaking together. They began to compete in contests, and soon they were able to share the memories of their wins and losses.

Another couple began to breed dogs and enter them in shows. Soon they shared proud moments when their dogs won. Their house was filled with ribbons and champion dog photos, each reminding them of a victorious moment, of an accomplishment from working together. They began to travel to shows across the country, discovering new places and making new friends.

If your marriage is boring and you don't have anything new to talk about, new friends can fill the bill. You can do things with them, then afterwards you can talk about them. New activities supply something to talk about as well as new people to talk to.

Do something exciting. Go on a balloon ride or a helicopter ride, or take a vacation somewhere you've never been before. Share a risk, but not necessarily a business venture. There are *some* things you should never share.

Dirty Dozen Dangerous Activities for Couples

1. GOING INTO BUSINESS TOGETHER—Most businesses fail, a strain your relationship can live without. But even if it's a successful business, the problems will spill into your private life.

2. BUILDING THE DREAM HOUSE—Every architect has a story about a couple who broke up over building a dream house. After many years of marriage, of saving and fantasizing, they can't agree on what they want. When they do agree, something goes wrong and they're upset. No real house can ever provide as much as they imagine it will. Buy, don't build.

3. HAVING AN OPEN MARRIAGE—Through the years I have known many couples who have tried a sexually open marriage. They have all broken up or stopped this difficult, if not impossible, lifestyle.

4. JOINING A CULT—The trouble with cults is that the organization is always more important than your relationship. Loyalties change from husband and wife to cult leader.

5. ILLEGAL ACTIVITIES—When either partner becomes involved in an illegal activity, the relationship is in danger. Doing something illegal involves lying, cheating and stealing, activities that can carry over into your relationship.

6. LONG SEPARATIONS—Few marriages can survive not being together over long periods of time.

7. VIOLENT ARGUMENTS—When you have violent arguments, you say and do things in the heat of anger that

can't be taken back. The other person remembers
what was said and it erodes their loving feelings.

8. SPENDING TOO MUCH TIME WITH SEPARATE ACTIVITIES—
   Couples who stay together spend lots of time together.
   You should spend a minimum of four hours a day
   with each other. Quality time doesn't make up for
   quantity of time.

9. ALWAYS BEING WITH OTHERS—Couples who are always
   in the company of other people, relatives, kids, friends
   and co-workers, can't be really intimate. Intimacy depends on spending time alone together.

10. CRITICISM—Couples who constantly criticize each
    other build resentment. Neither partner feels appreci-
    ated and togetherness is threatened.

11. CONSTANT CRISES—Although marriages can survive
    major tragedies, a state of constant uproar and crises
    can tear people apart.

12. WITHHOLDING—Not sharing feelings, letting things
    stew and fester until they become major problems, is
    destructive to intimacy and partnership.

Using Podium Effect

Just because you've been together a long time doesn't
mean that you can't get his attention and interest by using the
"podium effect." Respect and admiration are such important
parts of a relationship that we should take every opportunity to
increase them. The best way to get your mate to look at you
with renewed love and respect is to show him how much other
people admire you.

Often when I'm traveling around the country promoting
my books, my husband will fly to join me for a weekend.
There's always at least one weekend television show and he
comes along with me. He sees me being appreciated and he
hears the audience's applause. Even if someone is holding up

an applause sign in the back, my husband is always so proud of me afterwards.

Whenever possible, I try to get my husband to come to seminars, lectures and book signings. That way I get more mileage out of my time than just selling books. I let my husband see all those people listening to me. It helps keep him convinced of how valuable I am.

Consider inviting your husband next time you are on a panel or speaking at an event. Bring him to your company parties so he can see how well you relate to others. Take him to the playoffs for your bowling league; let him hear others applaud your efforts.

Have lots of your women friends over. Let him see how popular you are. Invite friends over for dinner and cook something wonderful. Let him hear their praise. Don't hide your accomplishments. Display them to others as well as to your mate. Let other people tell him how terrific you are. He'll be so impressed.

Repetition

Do you remember the old song, "You're getting to be a habit with me?" Well, that's what happens. You and your mate get to be a habit with each other. He gets used to having you there. You get accustomed to him. He doesn't sleep well if you're not there. He tosses and turns all night if you're out of town.

Love is indeed an addiction, an addiction to the other person. If you have your man properly addicted to you, it'll be really hard for him to break away. He can be addicted to your smell, the sound of your voice, the way you touch him, the sight of you, the way you read the paper together in the morning and the way you watch the television news last thing at night.

Just as he developed his other addictions, perhaps following the sports pages or needing two cups of black coffee every morning through repetition, he will develop an addiction to you through repetition. By doing something over and over again with the same person, you begin to associate the activity with the person. If you always shower together, he'll miss you if he has to shower alone. If you always eat together, he'll feel lonely if he has to eat alone.

Men are more easily addicted by repetition than women are. Men like their rituals and the security of knowing everything will be the same.

We've heard for years that men like, even need, variety. Not true. Men fall easily into a contented rhythm of domesticity. Men become addicted to sex with the same woman, not to different women. Men become addicted to the thrill of sneaking, if they get away with it. It's not the other woman they're addicted to.

It's important to make sex a habit with your mate. Have sex with him regularly, if only to reinforce his habit of getting all his pleasure from you. Make sure you spend regular times together. Make certain things de rigueur in your relationship: going to church every Sunday, renting a movie every Friday, having cocktails every evening, even watching a favorite television show together. The more rituals you have, the more totally intimate and involved you are as a couple and the more fun doing something "different" becomes.

Use repetition to reinforce the anchors you have set. Use it to trigger his love experience. Repeat pet sexy phrases. Play your favorite music over and over. Repeat your pet sayings and names for each other. Say "I love you" a lot. Say it in his Love Language. "See how much I love you (for the visual man)." Or, for the auditory man, "Let me tell you how much I love you." Or, for the feelings man "Can you feel my love?"

Murray, married to Rose for almost fifty years, told me, "I tell her I love her all the time. She tells me she loves me too." They have seven children, ages 17 to 47. "If I don't tell her I love her everyday, she says to me, 'What's the matter, Murray, is the honeymoon over?'"

You can never say I love you too often. Besides, the more you say it to him, the more he'll say it back.

Flattery

Long-married women all say, "Flatter him. Tell him he's wonderful." It always works, but what he really responds to is the constant repetition of the loving feelings he gets when you flatter him. Flattery from you is more important to your mate than from anyone else. Lay it on him.

I can hear the objections already. "Flatter him? That's as old as the hills." Well, maybe. But if you've read the latest management books like *The One-Minute Manager,* you will notice that the advice is the same. Look for something your employees are doing right and then flatter them. Give them the one-minute praising, complete with a touch, in case you have a feelings employee.

Men have been going to seminars and learning the one-minute manager advice as well as other management techniques. Then, you can be sure, they come home and try them on their wives. I've even caught my husband using a couple on me that come right out of his latest manual. You might as well use these same techniques on your household that your mate is using in his office—and probably at home as well.

Using flattery and repetition is especially effective if you can find something to flatter him about that nobody but you really appreciates—perhaps the way he is so patient and sweet with the kids, or maybe the way he helps his parents with a problem. One favorite thing men love to hear is, "You were right about . . ." Surely you can find something he was right about.

Drug addicts come back again and again to their drugs because they know they can get predictable, repeatable pleasure on demand. If you use repetition and take advantage of the addictive qualities of love, your man will always come back to you, his dependable, predictable, repeatable source of pleasure.

20

Rekindling the Flame

AS I wrote this book, I found it hard to resist the temptation to make every possible thing in my own marriage perfect right now, and to get my way on every issue. After talking to many couples about their problems, I was worried about having those same problems in my marriage thirty years from now.

Then I would remember my interviews with older couples at a nearby retirement community. I talked to them on the golf course, in the health club, everywhere! I was amazed at how well they got along.

I watched an older couple. He helped her out of her chair, handed her her cane and walked away. She followed him. It was an automatic gesture, something they had done for years. I asked her, "Aren't you upset that he doesn't wait for you, that he just hands you your cane and walks away?"

"No, dear," she told me. "He's going to pay the bill and get the car. That's how we always do it."

As I spent time watching these couples and talking to them, I began to get a new perspective on my own marriage. Suddenly I saw us growing old together, helping each other out of chairs, passing the cane or pushing the walker.

Looking at our lives from a long-range point of view made every problem shrink. The everyday problems and compromises, the disagreement over what movie to see or what to have for dinner or what to let the kids do or not do seem much smaller when you have a larger view of marriage. By imagining ourselves growing old together, we can see that what we do this weekend doesn't seem so important when we think about all the weekends we are going to have together.

Marriage Exercises

Visualize you and your partner together as you grow older and older. Imagine what you're going to look like, how your life will be as the years go by. Picture the two of you gray and wrinkled, retired, sitting side by side in rocking chairs. Perhaps you're working in the garden, maybe he's snoozing in the sun.

One of the main components in marriages that last is this long-range viewpoint. Couples who stay together "till death do us part" are couples who can see themselves together forever. You can't achieve any goal you can't imagine. Achieving a long-lasting relationship is like any other goal—you must visualize it. You must imagine yourself achieving it.

Imagine the peaceful feeling you'll have knowing you're secure in each other's love. Tell yourself: "My husband (insert name) and I will be together forever. I see us getting old together. I imagine our two wrinkled hands still close, our graying heads side by side. I will always be there for (insert name). My husband (insert name) will always be there for me."

When you think of your marriage as a lifelong commitment, you realize not everything is so important. If you don't get your way this time, you may next time. You decide not to battle over everything. You are more willing to compromise on issues.

Keeping Romance Alive

Romantic love came into being during the Dark Ages of our civilization. It flourished at a time when knights worshiped ladies from afar. Romantic love was only for the noblemen of the time, not for the peasants. Romantic love, as originally conceived, was meant to be enjoyed from afar, and never consummated. Certainly you didn't make love, marry and have children with someone about whom you were having romantic thoughts. It was only when the peasants adapted romantic love from the noblemen that the essence of romance was tarnished by the intrusions of everyday life.

Romantic love was meant for Lancelot and Guinevere, for Romeo and Juliet, not for Sam and Sally and Bob and Barbara. Romantic love was meant to be thwarted, to be hope and fantasies and dreams, not reality. Romance was meant for imagination, not real life. So is it any wonder that we yearn for that part of romance that is separate from lust, that is pure and untarnished like one perfect rose? It is always there, but it changes throughout a relationship.

The Stages of a Relationship

THE BEGINNING

We feel romantic love most strongly in the first stages of our relationship. We are overwhelmed by it, obsessed with thoughts of the man who has taken control of our mind. Romance flourishes when we can't have quite as much of the other person as we want, when we yearn constantly for more, when we need to possess their being, their essence, their heart and soul. Romantic love needs obstacles to overcome, trials to survive. Romantic love needs fantasy, so we can imagine that other person to be so much more beautiful, more intelligent, more perfect than they really are.

SECOND STAGE OF LOVE

When we move to commitment, we're ready to overcome the obstacles, to admit that we really want to be with that other person and no other. And when he agrees, guess what? Romantic love immediately starts to fade. Suddenly it's pushed aside by everyday life, by who left the cap off the toothpaste and must you always put the toilet paper on the roll backwards?

The instant that romantic love is consummated—not necessarily sexually, but emotionally—it begins to suffer. Since the man no longer has to wonder whether he'll one day have his love object, one of the major ingredients of romantic love is missing. Suddenly you're doing all kinds of unromantic things together where before you only did romantic things. Now you have to worry about closet space and laundry and bills and cooking and cleaning. Your time together is no longer just evenings out and candlelight and soft music.

Suddenly you discover marriage and commitment is not like one long date. Actually, you spent more quality time together when you were dating. You're upset and you wonder where the romance went. He never brings you flowers anymore. You don't cook with candlelight and negligees. You wonder if you're sinking into an abyss of babies, budgets and bills.

Actually, hardly anyone's romantic stage lasts longer than five years, whether they date, marry or live together. Five years seems to be the cutoff period for keeping the "in-love" feeling alive. One reason is that in order for the in-love feeling to flourish there has to be insecurity. Hardly anyone still feels insecure after five years of living together.

THE THIRD STAGE

This is when the bloom is definitely off the rose. The romance has been missing for a long time. You begin to realize he has lots of faults you didn't know were there. He decides he can't stand the traits in you he used to think were cute.

You wonder if you really can spend the rest of your life with him and his problems. You begin to think about having an affair. You wonder if he is.

You are both rebelling against the compromises you make,

often pulling in opposite directions. You begin to wonder about the road not taken, the dreams not achieved and whether your partner has kept you from realizing them. When you're up and happy, he's not. When he's happy, you're not.

You are both struggling to be in charge of yourselves, the relationship, your lives and your future. The only thing that gets you through this stage is lots of romantic memories to fall back on. You hang in because you know it can be better.

THE FOURTH STAGE

You decide you care about each other in spite of all the things you saw wrong with each other in the third stage. You decide you might just grow old together. You have survived kid problems, money problems, career problems, ego problems and sex problems. You begin to take care of each other in a way you never did before.

THE FIFTH STAGE

Nothing, except an act of God, can separate you now.

Lots of the couples I interviewed had reached the fifth stage of their relationship. Some had been married fifteen years, some fifty, but they were locked together by the many things they had in common, like two adjoining pieces of a jigsaw puzzle, different, yet fitting perfectly.

Appreciation Not Criticism

All of the couples in the fifth stage of their relationship praised each other often and undauntedly.

Looking for something to praise is an important management technique. Sometimes just writing down the good things about your mate can rekindle love's flame.

LIST—WONDERFUL QUALITIES
MY HUSBAND HAS

1. *He's intelligent*   ) *avoids arguments*
2. *He's handsome*   ) *hobbies*
3. *He's patient*   ) *Compromises*
4. *He's gentle*
5. *He's Understanding*
6. *He's has a good humor.*
7. *A good job.*
8. *He enjoys working out (limit)*
9. *He can cook*
10. *And is sometimes romantic*
    He challenges me

If you don't love yourself, you make it hard for him to love you.

LIST—WONDERFUL THINGS ABOUT ME

1. *I'm attractive* ✓
2. *Understanding*
3. *good humor*
4. *A love life*
5. *Thankful for life →*
6. *Flexible*
7. *Many hobbies*
8. *Come from a close family*
9. *good outlook a future*
10. *Talented*

It's important to think of your man in terms of other "real" men you know, instead of comparing him to some fictional

Prince Charming who only exists in romance books and fantasies.

LIST—THINGS I'M LUCKY
HE DOESN'T DO

1. _drugs_
2. _abuse me_
3. _doesn't sleep around_
4. _not a maniac_
5. _doesn't raise his voice_
6. _be lazy_
7. _____
8. _____
9. _____
10. _____

LIST—THINGS HE'S LUCKY
I DON'T DO

1. _sleep around_
2. _drugs_
3. _____
4. _____
5. _____
6. _____
7. _____
8. _____
9. _____
10. _____

Men are always complaining that they want to be romantic, they just don't understand what we want. The following page is for him. You may want to add a few things of your own at the bottom.

List—What's Romantic, What's Not
(Tear out and give page to husband)

 1. Being alone together, just the two of us, is romantic. Being with other people is not.

 2. A wonderful, unexpected, extravagant gift is romantic. A new vacuum cleaner is not.

 3. Flowers from the florist are romantic. Steaks from the meat market are not.

 4. Eating out is romantic. Eating at home is not.

 5. Fancy restaurants are romantic, cafeterias and buffets are not.

 6. Walking in the park at sunset is romantic. Jogging at dawn is not.

 7. Staying overnight at a hotel with room service is romantic. Motel 6 is not.

 8. Long, ambling scenic drives are romantic. Rushing through traffic is not.

 9. Staying at a country inn is romantic. Going on an incentive trip or to a convention is not.

10. Talking over breakfast is romantic. Reading the papers is not.

11. Fancy cocktails, fine wine and champagne are romantic. Beer is not.

12. Window shopping at Gucci's is romantic. Browsing at the auto supply store is not.

13. Being swept away is romantic. Stopping for gas is not.

14. Love letters are romantic. Reminder notes are not.

15. Looking through old photos is romantic. Sorting bills is not.

16. Art, the ballet, poetry are romantic. Boxing, off-road racing and *Playboy* magazine are not.

17. Old movies and love stories are romantic. Shoot-'em-ups and horror flicks are not.

18. Going away is romantic. Taking the kids is not.

19. Surprises are romantic. The same old thing is not.

20. Soft music is romantic. Football and baseball games are not.

21. Telling me how good I look is romantic. Saying how good some other woman looks is not.

22. SAYING I LOVE YOU IS. SAYING YOU SMELL ISN'T

23. Dreaming together is. Knocking worms is not.

24. _____

25. _____

LIST—WHAT'S SEXY, WHAT'S NOT

1. Satin sheets are sexy. New sheets are sexy. Beautiful sheets are sexy. Old striped sheets are not.

2. Hot tubs and bubble baths and long showers together are sexy. Going to bed funky is not.

3. Making love with soft lights and music is sexy. Making love while "60 Minutes" is on is not.

4. Massages with scented oils are sexy. Having your back popped is not.

5. Reading erotic poetry is sexy. *Hustler* is not.

6. Being all alone for a weekend is sexy. Having people around is not.

7. Being taken out to dinner first is sexy. Being thrown down for a quickie is not.

8. Undressing each other slowly is sexy. Making love with your socks on is not.

9. Finding body parts to admire is sexy. Finding cellulite is not.

10. Making love in a strange place is sexy. Making love where you can hear the phone is not.

11. _Caressing is sexy, hitting is not_

12. _____

13. _____

14. _____

15. _____

Romantic Getaways

When couples come to me for counseling, I often recommend a romantic getaway. It can make their problems disappear like magic. "Sure," I tell them, "you can have a candlelit dinner for two at home, but somehow a change of scenery makes it more romantic. Besides, with both your busy schedules, you're lucky to gulp side-by-side TV dinners."

Sometimes couples are worried about the money or time away from other obligations. But I tell them, "Consider it an investment in your relationship. Romantic memories are very important for the rest of your lives."

Quality time is not just for parents and kids. It's for husbands and wives, too. The big question is, can you have quality time together when you're about to be interrupted at any moment by the telephone, the doorbell, the kids or an inoperative modern convenience? Even if you're not really interrupted, just the threat of it can mar the greatest romantic intentions.

To be really romantic, you sometimes have to escape to a place where nobody calls you "Mom," where everything works, where every sunset can be enjoyed, where candlelight glows softly, where telephones don't ring and where lifelong memories can be made.

RULES FOR ROMANTIC GETAWAYS

1. Write ahead for brochures to both the hotel and the local area chamber of commerce or pick up some from your travel agent. Look them over together. This gives you time to fantasize together before you even leave home. Just thinking about getting away can make you feel better.

2. Let him eliminate some places. Choose the place together. That way, nobody blames anybody else if they don't like it. Find out everything about the place before you go.

3. When you make your reservation, find out about the room you're going to stay in. Get confirmed reservations, including your room. Specify beach or ocean front if that's what you want. Find out about the view. Ask if they have anything special, maybe a fireplace or hot tub for two. Some of the most fabulous romantic destinations have some rooms that are better than others for just a few more dollars.

4. Don't scrimp on your romantic getaway. This is an investment in your future.

5. Before you leave, make a list of all the projects and things you need to do around the house, the errands you have to run, the work you've left undone. That way you get it all off your mind before you leave. Arrange for a reliable friend to handle anything unexpected that might come up while you're away. Then forget everything.

6. Go over the ground rules: No bickering over old battles. No worrying about diets. No worrying about kids, in-laws, or work.

7. Take recreational reading. No briefcases, business books, reports, or work.

8. Don't overplan. Allow plenty of time for just laying around and enjoying each other.

9. Tell everybody you don't want to hear from them while you're away and not to expect postcards.

10. Take your favorite music, sex toys and even a favorite pillow. Take candles, incense or your very own scent to spray around the room, and special bubble baths.

11. Don't plan to look up old friends or visit long-lost relatives or have just one business meeting on your trip.

12. Say "I love you" every morning and every night.

Erasing Old Messages

One of the real dangers to your relationship is the old messages you may have that keep you from loving without fear of loss or rejection. Many of the women who come to my workshops have deep-seated fears and terrible old messages that stand in the way of enjoying their relationships:

"Maybe he doesn't love me anymore."

"Maybe he's got someone on the side."

"I'm too fat (ugly, skinny, tall, short, etcetera) to be loved."

"He'd love me more if I was a blonde.

"Maybe he's going to get hit by a truck today and I'll never see him again."

These are just some of the definitely not-true messages women have carried around. Even the most beautiful, the most successful women, have heads that reel with terrible thoughts about themselves. I have developed a speedy and effective way of erasing those messages.

By combining physical exercise and affirmations, the messages will disappear. It's a matter of reprogramming your own mind. Instead of counting steps or counting leg kicks, say an affirmation with each leg kick, or a word per step. Affirmations should be repeated over and over again, like a prayer or a mantra. Whenever the doubtful phrase starts to haunt you, replace it with the positive affirmation. If you say your affirmation enough times, you will smother the defeating thoughts out of your mind.

Affirmations should be simple and easy to remember. Try, "I am beautiful" or "I am lovable." Try, "(Insert name) loves me" or "I love (insert name)." In a way, repeating positive affirmations over and over again, especially while you're exercising, is self-brainwashing. When you combine your affirmations with a sudden rush of oxygen to your brain from exercising, plus the physically intensive experience, you can get almost immediate benefits. You'll be more loving and more lovable without those old messages.

Tell yourself you deserve happiness. See yourself getting all the joy in life you want. Feel the sweet vibes of love pass through you and encompass everyone around you.

21

Staying Sexy

I S sex important? You bet! Is it the most important part of your relationship? Hardly. Can you live without it? Sure. Do you want to? Probably not.

When He's Hot and You're Not

Suddenly you've lost interest in sex. You don't care if you never do it again. It's too hot, or too cold. Or you have a backache, or you're worried about the kids or the bills or the living-room ceiling.

You need to turn yourself back on. Being sexually awake and alive is important to your relationship, it's important to your connection with the world, it's important to your energy level and your basic psyche. A sexually dead person is on the way to being old.

I've heard all the excuses in the world: "He's lost his appeal. He just doesn't turn me on anymore" is the most popular one.

. Surprise! It's not his job to turn you on. It's yours. You're supposed to turn yourself on.

261

When you suddenly lose interest in sex, you really lose touch with your body. You begin to feel undesirable and unlovable. You put out undesirable, unlovable vibes—and guess what happens? The man in your life begins to think you are undesirable and unlovable, just like you do.

First Aid for Not Feeling Sexy

1. Emphasize your good points.

If you don't feel attractive and sexy, you won't be attractive and sexy. Forget the old advice about standing naked in front of a mirror for five minutes and just concentrating on your positive points. If you feel fat, you're just going to look at the fat, even if it's invisible to everyone else. The way to feel desirable and sexy is to begin making small parts of your body beautiful. Start with something easy to control: your nails, your feet, your hands, your hair, your makeup, your clothes.

Everyone has one terrific feature—great eyes, a beautiful mouth, elegant hands or tiny, perfectly shaped feet. Concentrate on your best feature. If it's your lips, go out and buy some new lipsticks, lip conditioners, lip liners, lip glosses. If it's your eyes, take loving care of them. Tenderly smooth cream around them, condition them, put drops in them, let them know they're loved. Buy them some new colored shadows, mascaras and liners. Take them for a makeover. Practice flirting with them in the mirror.

I have a friend who is terribly overweight but she has terrific legs and tiny feet. She always wears very expensive high heels, strappy sandals in bright young colors, and even has a diamond imbedded in one tiny pink toenail. On her ankle dances a butterfly embossed in her stockings. At parties, she daintily crosses her shapely legs and her husband hasn't taken his eyes off her legs in years. "I make love in a mumu," she confided in me once. "We have a special position where Sam holds my feet and kisses them while we make love. He just loves my feet. At first, I didn't think it was sexy, but now I do. I love it when Sam rubs my feet and kisses them."

What is it your man loves about you? Your hair, your lips, your hands, legs, feet, breasts, butt? Surely you know.

2. Wear something sexy.

It's true. Just putting on lacy undies instead of the old ones with the yellowed elastic will make you feel sexier. Buy sheer stockings instead of support hose. Wear a lace bra instead of the old cotton one. Buy a sheer flowy nightgown instead of a flannel one this year.

Even Montgomery Ward and Sears sell sexy nightgowns and bathrobes. You don't have to go to a sleazy sex store or even face a saleswoman who wonders why you want a garter belt and black stockings.

Look in the back of *Playgirl* or *Cosmopolitan* or even *Ms.* Notice the ads for catalogues from Frederick's of Hollywood or Adam and Eve or Victoria's Secrets or Xandria. Send away for the catalogues.

When they come, set aside some time to look through them. Order something outrageous or just get turned on imagining what you would do with some of the silly, sexy stuff, like candy panties. You'll find everything from Joy Jell to lovecuffs, satin to leather, feathers to vibrators.

3. Buy a vibrator.

This is a must for the modern woman. Yes, your orgasm is your own responsibility. If you can't give yourself one, how do you expect him to give you one? A woman's most exquisitely exciting spot is still the clitoris. I recommend a plug-in type vibrator. The Panasonic Panabrator or Prelude Three (sold in catalogues above) or even a Sears model with tiny rubber attachments are all good. Use the hard rubber knob, not the one with the little rubber fingers.

Real men don't mind vibrators. As a matter of fact, they're

happy to have this modern sexual accoutrement as a part of their normal bedroom activity. As one man told me, "I'd sure rather have my wife vibrate herself while we make love than not come at all."

One important reason the missionary position is not all it's cracked up to be is because it's difficult for the woman to stimulate her clitoris during sex in this position. Doggy style or almost any other position allows clitoral stimulation.

Practice masturbating with your vibrator when nobody's home. Then, you'll be able to come with quicker predictability when you're having sex. The more you come, the more you will be able to come. You won't wear out or run out of juices.

You may also want to have a battery-operated vibrator for travel in foreign countries.

4. Fantasize.

Read sexy books and imagine you're the main character. Don't worry if the fantasy that turns you on doesn't live up to your expectations of who you are. I've had women tell me they're embarrassed because what really turns them on are books like *The Story of O,* a story of a relationship where the woman is a slave. Or, they're embarrassed because they're turned on by imagining being raped by swarms of pirates, or bikers. That's why romance books sell so well—they all have fantasy sex scenes. Romance readers report better, not worse, sex lives, simply because they think about sex so much when they read those books.

Sex and romance are really tied together, and your brain is still the most potent sex organ, so don't deny your fantasies. Read best sellers like *Lucky* or *Hollywood Wives,* books by Judith Krantz or Sidney Sheldon, or lusty romance novels. Think about sex. Shop for sexy clothes. (You don't have to buy any, but it does get you in the mood to try them on.) Send for something sexy in a mail-order catalogue. Read books about sex. The more you think about sex, the sexier you will become.

5. Go somewhere sexy.

No matter what anybody says, home is not as sexy as other places. You can take a long, sensual bubble bath at home, you can even masturbate at home, but sometimes you need some new stimulus to get started. Get out of the house. Go to a sexy movie. Go somewhere with sexual vibes—perhaps a gym with lots of single members or a racquetball club or a very chic restaurant or a club with male dancers.

When You're Hot and He's Not

It's not uncommon. Even young couples have problems. No matter what "Dear Abby" says, if it doesn't work, it doesn't work, and no amount of nagging or cajoling will get most husbands to a sex therapist. If your sex life is in trouble, it's going to be up to you to do something about it. Probably, your mate can't even talk to you about it, so you know even talking to him about talking to a stranger is out of the question. You worry that bringing up the subject will create more stress, anger, and ultimately no sex.

Here are some tried-and-true tips for seducing your man. I call them "Tips from the Pros," because that's where I got them.

Once, I spent several weeks traveling around the country investigating prostitution for a large men's magazine. The magazine had lots of questions, but *I* was curious about one thing: How come they were getting paid for it and I could hardly give it away? What were their secrets? I wondered. After hundreds of interviews with women who were no prettier than me (but somehow men panted after them like dogs in heat), I began to get the picture. The men were seduced by the *promise* of sex.

TIPS FROM THE PROS

1. Give good phone.

The women who made the most money were not necessarily the prettiest, they were the best promisers. They were on the phone from early morning until late at night, cooing and billing, talking sweet nothings about how much they missed the client, wondering what he was doing with his sexy self. The women who had the most happy regulars gave great phone.

Seduce your man by calling him and making a date for sex. Talk in a soft, sweet voice. Let him know how much you'll be looking forward to your time together. Pretend you're going to get $500 an hour. He'll be thinking about it all day long.

2. Spend time getting ready.

Don't let him see the preparations.

Many women whose husbands are getting lots of perfectly good sex at home are shocked to find out their man had a fling with a sex-for-pay lady of the evening. What's he getting that he doesn't get at home? they wonder. The truth is: probably very little, except the presentation is different.

Buy something new and frilly. Prepare for him as if he were your biggest customer. Wash your hair, do your nails, get a full body massage. Look good when he gets there.

3. Respond.

The sexiest thing a woman can do is be responsive to her man. Let him know he turns you on.

4. Give him your full attention.

Listening is one of the sexiest things a big money-making call girl does.

5. Find out his fantasy, and be it.

Is there a reasonable sex act he's just dying to try? Could you see it in your heart to give him the experience?

6. Try to be the best he's ever had. . . . So he always wants more.

Big Lies About Sex and Love

Over the years we've all heard what we should or shouldn't do in the bedroom to keep our men happy. Much of what we've been told just isn't so.

1. You have to be available to make love whenever he wants, even when you're not in the mood.

You absolutely shouldn't force yourself to make love when you don't feel like it. Of course, there's nothing wrong with trying to get in the mood, but you can keep your man in love without having sex whenever he wants. Never turn down his advances, though, without a promise of future sex. Sexual stimulus is the expectation of sexual pleasure. In other words, a man is turned on if he thinks he's going to get sexual pleasure. So one of the best ways to keep a man interested and excited is always promise him, even when you have a headache, that eventually, something wonderful is going to happen for him.

Don't just push him away or tell him you're not in the mood; always give a promise of future delights. You don't have to make love if you don't feel like it, but you should let him know he's still desirable and you'll be hot for him later. That way, even when you turn him down, you leave him turned on.

2. Sex should just happen spontaneously.

Waiting for spontaneous sex to occur can make a long exasperating dry spell even longer. Today's two-career couples are sometimes lucky to meet over TV dinners. Plan sex encounters way ahead of time. Spend time getting ready and thinking about it. Then you both have time to build up lots of sexual expectations. Even though we all want our lovemaking to be spontaneous, planned sex is better than no sex at all.

Make a date with your man. Don't break it for any reason. Plan an evening or afternoon out that ends with sex.

3. Men just want sex.

Men want more than sex. Let him know you love him. Touch him a lot, even when there's no chance of sex at the moment. Nonsexual touching leads to sexual touching. Even when it doesn't lead to sex, touching stimulates the feelings part of a man and gives him pleasure. If you want your man to hang around you all the time, you should be the source of his physical pleasure. Even when you don't feel like sex, you can hug and kiss him and let him know you love him.

4. All men are alike.

Don't compare. Your girl friend says she and her husband have sex "six times a week, doesn't everybody?" You begin to think your perfectly good twice a week, or even once every other week, is a bummer. Every relationship has its own rhythm. So does yours.

Also, beware of comparing your relationship to an imaginary one where an exciting and dangerous man with an eye patch and a mysterious foreign accent sweeps you off your feet and into the night. Remember, it's hard to have exciting and reliable in the same man.

5. You can't teach an old mate new tricks.

You can definitely get your man to do something different in bed. Encourage him when he shows any signs of doing what you want. Don't criticize. If you want more afterplay, instigate it. Kiss him, cuddle him, and when he finally kisses you back, say, "Oh, it makes me feel so good when you're so romantic." Reinforce him with praise when he does something right, even if you have to instigate it or exaggerate how well he does.

Let him know you're pleased when he does something that feels good.

6. Men want sex all the time.

Not all men want sex all the time. Always test the waters first. Make sure the time is right. Make sure he's in the mood. Don't push him to have sex when he seems tired, uninterested, or preoccupied.

7. Bad sex is better than no sex.

No sex is better for your relationship than a bad sex experience. Impotence is compounded by more impotence. Primary impotence (not getting it up) gets compounded by secondary impotence (fear of not getting it up). Frigidity (not coming) is compounded by fear of frigidity.

8. Men like sexually aggressive women.

Men like women who flirt, who tease, who titillate just a little. Then they want the woman to step back and let them take over. Mostly, men want women to be just aggressive enough to assure them they won't be rejected. Men don't like women who try to take over the aggressive role totally.

9. It's okay if you don't come, as long as he does.

No, it's not okay. Not for you, not for him. Most men report their primary satisfaction comes from both their own orgasms and their ability to give pleasure to their mates.

10. You shouldn't do it the same way all the time.

When couples have been together for a long time, they develop a sense of security about a certain sex act or a certain series of sex acts that always gives them pleasure. Sure, it's fun to try something different once in a while, or to do it in a strange place, but there's nothing like holding that same old body in the same old way to give you that same old feeling.

11. Quickies don't count.

Quickies are perfectly acceptable. It's better to have a quickie than nothing at all. Quickies hold you over until you have time for longer lovemaking.

12. Older couples have lots of great sex.

"Not everything gets harder as you get older," lamented one woman married forty-six years.

"I wish we'd had more sex when we were younger," another woman, married fifty-three years, told me.

"Nothing lasts forever," smiled another.

We hear lots about how sex can stay hot as long as we want, how you can make love forever. But according to the women I've interviewed and the surveys I've taken, it just doesn't last forever. That's one good reason to enjoy as much good sex as you can while you and your mate are both able, interested, and turned on.

Women who've been married a long time confide in me that they don't have those delicious, tingly surges of lust as often for the men they loved. If once they couldn't keep their hands off each other, and they couldn't wait to consummate their love in mad, passionate encounters, now they reach for each other with less lust. Their hearts don't beat nearly as fast as they once did at a mere touch. They feel more secure. Jealousy, anxiety and fear have waned, and sometimes passion and drama too. These feelings are replaced by devotion and companionship, shared interests, friends and relatives, and a deep and secure love.

Many of the women I interviewed told me they had accepted the fact that passion would not burn forever. They said they knew that it was foolish to hang on to romantic dreams and remember the fairytale fantasies of their youth where the handsome prince swept them off their feet to live happily ever after.

And then a certain look would creep into their eyes, a soft

look, a secret glow that softened their features and made them suddenly beautiful, no matter what their age.

"Just when you think it's all over," one woman in her sixties told me, "just when you think the passion has turned to compassion, he will look at you a certain way, or touch you the way he used to, or call your name a certain way, and it will all come rushing back. And you're surprised because the passion, the heat, the sweetness of his smile still sends shivers down your spine and you know it'll never die as long as you live."